# The Geography of the Port of London

*The Geography of the Port of London* (1957) deals with the mid-century functions of the port studied in relation to their physical setting and in the light of their historical development. An analysis of the roles of the various dock and wharf systems is followed by a discussion of the present commerce of the port, illustrated by post-war statistics. The multiple background to this activity is also presented, including a discussion of the 1950s physical condition of the River Thames and of the markets and industries associated with the port. It presents a comprehensive picture of this at-the-time greatest British seaport, considered with reference to certain principles of economic geography.

# The Geography of the Port of London

James Bird

Routledge
Taylor & Francis Group

First published in 1957
by Hutchinson University Library

This edition first published in 2025 by Routledge
4 Park Square, Milton Park, Abingdon, Oxon, OX14 4RN

and by Routledge
605 Third Avenue, New York, NY 10017

*Routledge is an imprint of the Taylor & Francis Group, an informa business*

© 1957 Hutchinson University Library

**Publisher's Note**
The publisher has gone to great lengths to ensure the quality of this reprint but points out that some imperfections in the original copies may be apparent.

**Disclaimer**
The publisher has made every effort to trace copyright holders and welcomes correspondence from those they have been unable to contact.

A Library of Congress record exists under LCCN a 58008617

ISBN: 978-1-032-91542-5 (hbk)
ISBN: 978-1-003-56381-5 (ebk)
ISBN: 978-1-032-91547-0 (pbk)

Book DOI 10.4324/9781003563815

# THE GEOGRAPHY OF THE PORT
## OF LONDON

HUTCHINSON UNIVERSITY LIBRARY

*GEOGRAPHY*

EDITORS:
*PROFESSOR S. W. WOOLDRIDGE, C.B.E., D.Sc.*
*and*
*PROFESSOR W. G. EAST, M.A.*
Professors of Geography in the University of London

# THE GEOGRAPHY OF
# THE PORT OF LONDON

JAMES BIRD
B.A., PH.D.
LECTURER IN GEOGRAPHY,
UNIVERSITY OF LONDON KING'S COLLEGE

HUTCHINSON UNIVERSITY LIBRARY

LONDON

HUTCHINSON UNIVERSITY LIBRARY
*178–202 Great Portland Street, London, W.1*

London Melbourne Sydney
Auckland Bombay Toronto
Johannesburg New York

★

*First published 1957*

*Set in ten point Times New Roman, one point
leaded, and printed in Great Britain
by The Anchor Press, Ltd.,
Tiptree, Essex*

To
O. J., K., & F. C. M.

# CONTENTS

CONTENTS

# LIST OF MAPS AND DIAGRAMS

[1] Based on a P.L.A. drawing by kind permission.

# PREFACE

A<small>NY</small> investigation which comes under the general heading of human geography depends very much on the co-operation of the men on the spot. In this case I was more than fortunate. At each step the most courteous welcome and help were received. It would be impossible to acknowledge all the assistance which has been given. May those who remember my questions turn to the section of this book which has been based on their answers and not be too dissatisfied.

My special thanks are due to C. F. J. Tomlinson, Esq., Chief Information Officer of the P.L.A., and E. W. King, Esq. (also of the P.L.A. Information Department); B. Stewart, Esq., P.L.A. Librarian, and his assistant, A. D. Simmons, Esq.; G. E. Tonge, Esq., Managing Director of the Proprietors of Hay's Wharf Ltd.; and, finally, the superintendents of each of the five dock systems and the assistant superintendents of each of the three Royal Docks whom I met during 1955 and 1956. Field work was also assisted by a grant from the Central Research Fund of the University of London.

Without the aid which has been so generously offered this book could not have been written. Yet in no sense is it an official publication. What is written remains my own responsibility.

Much help and encouragement have been received from the editors of this series; the final typed version of the text and much of the proof-reading have been carried out by my wife; and the diagrams have been prepared with the aid of the technical staff of the Joint School of Geography of King's College, London, and the London School of Economics and Political Science. To all these I extend my grateful thanks.

*University of London King's College.*

11

# CHAPTER I

# INTRODUCTION: SITUATION AND SITE

THE inclusion of the word 'geography' in the title of this book needs explanation if the terms of reference are to be clear. The geography of a port might be expected to deal merely with the arrangement and relative position of its component parts. Such a task could be simplified into a detailed map with a long index. This would serve a useful gazetteer purpose and answer the question 'Where?'; but the questions 'When?', 'How?', and, most importantly, 'Why?' would be left unanswered. The observer who sees a port merely as a collection of docks, quays, wharves, and warehouses misses the fundamental quality of such a place. There are some littorals today, and there were more in the past, possessing no such installations; passengers and goods are unloaded offshore into small boats and landed at some hazard across open water, even through rolling surf. Where this is regularly done, such landing places are rightly called ports, for they are the gateways between sea and land.

Apart from the variety of natural landing places, ports may be constructed out into the sea. These 'land-encroaching' ports thrust out their moles to create a harbour within; in other ports the land is excavated and the water encroaches. The more highly developed the port, the more artificial and elongated becomes the line of contact between land and water. This is desirable because it is the function of the port to effect exchanges between the traffic on these two elements; the longer the boundary between them, the greater is the opportunity for transhipment. Such illustration shows that any attempt to define ports by an inherent character-istic of form is impossible.[1]

It is much more convenient to define a port in terms of its function rather than in terms of its form. Of course, a thorough description of the port's traffic entails a consideration of the immediate destination or origin of the passengers and cargo. Their journey close to the port on land or across the sea approaches to the port affects the manner in which they are moved to and from the land. Nevertheless, the closer the observer is to the place of the actual movement of men and goods over a ship's side, the closer he is to the place where the essential function of the port is carried out.

If this is borne in mind, it becomes possible to delimit the terms of reference for this study, even when confronted by the formidable complications of the Port of London. The essential task is to trace the development of those areas where the function of transhipment is carried out. The complicated forms of this transhipment function will suggest that it is impossible to make precise linear limits to the port. This fact must be recognized at the outset.

It may be pointed out that the Port of London Authority (hereafter called the P.L.A.) has jurisdiction by Act of Parliament over areas with definite limits (see Appendix). Yet no one could claim that the P.L.A. administers the whole Port of London. The wharves along the banks of the river are outside its jurisdiction, and the chief markets which help to control the movement of goods are equally independent. A full examination of the markets of London is obviously outside the scope of this book. Yet there are certain markets which deserve to be considered in the light of the part they play in assisting the movement of goods through the port. Moreover, many of the bulk cargoes landed on the banks of Lower Thameside are destined for riverside industries. A treatment of the Port of London which did not include a discussion of the industrial development of Lower Thameside would be manifestly incomplete.

A study of the dock systems is easier to define because the docks are all bounded by a customs fence. Here the port function is limited in a most palpable way in the landward direction. Yet, as will be seen, the dock areas are very discontinuous, split up into five major systems. It is their common function which unites them under the P.L.A.

Dock systems, wharves, markets, industries, and movements to and from these are therefore on the agenda. One vital topic needs to be added—the water approach. Here the P.L.A. holds undisputed sway since it is the conservator of the whole tidal Thames from just below Teddington to the beginning of the Outer Estuary. Strictly speaking, this study, as titled, ought to examine all features of the port function along the whole of the tidal Thames and along the contiguous rivers and waterways within the region of Greater London. However, the emphasis will be lightened inland from the Thames and upstream of Brentford, for there much of the movement of goods partakes of the nature of inland waterway traffic.

This is the theme so far put forward. The constituent parts of the Port of London are held together by a common function, although their individual forms are varied and discontinuous. The price paid in taking this point of view is the inability to put a definite line around the subject. This is not serious. Though customs fences do exist in the port, lines conceived to be drawn across the movement of passengers and cargo are an impediment to an understanding of the port's operation.

Before embarking upon the points of the agenda outlined above, the physical environment and the history of the port must be discussed. This is the assignment in the rest of this chapter and in the chapter which follows. Without such background knowledge many features of the present scene are inexplicable; with such knowledge the port today is seen as a development of the potentialities of its situation and site by generations of men who have worked to make it what it is.

An important task in geography is the elucidation of the physiographic stage upon which man has erected his own scenery. The nature of the physical environment does not determine the use which man shall make of it; its influence varies from place to place and at different times in the same place. It is difficult to generalize about its role except to say that the influence of the physical setting is likely to be strongest in the earliest days of its use, because the smaller the number of people and the less developed their technology, the more they are likely to be influenced by the natural advantages and disadvantages of their immediate environment.

Two approaches are necessary. There is a need to see the *general* physical setting of the port; secondly, the physical *details* of the port in its early days should be examined when the influence of the physical environment is likely to be strongest. Terms to describe these two approaches may be borrowed from those who have made a special study of urban geography.

'On maps of large scale the relation between the internal pattern of the city . . . and the features of the terrain are analysed : on maps of smaller scale covering a much larger area the external relations of the city as a whole are analysed. The close-up view reveals the characteristics of the site ; the broader view reveals the characteristics of the situation.'[2]

'. . . the site . . . may be defined as the ground upon which a town stands, the area of earth it actually occupies . . . and as such is only part of a much wider setting. . . . This brings us to the conception of the situation of a town, its position in relation to its surroundings.'[3]

In urban geography these special uses of the words 'situation' and 'site' may be taken as established. Yet if the town which is studied is also a port, a duplication of these conceptions is necessary ; the land situation and site must be supplemented by a view of the water situation and site.

SITUATION

The land situation of the Port of London is primarily the London Basin, a syncline, or downfold, of Chalk which emerges in the north as the Chiltern Hills and in the south as the North Downs. The syncline has a gentler upward slope to the north, and since it pitches towards the North Sea, the tracts of Chalk diverge from one another in that direction. In this basin deposits of Tertiary age and later have been accumulated, and the chief artery of drainage is the Thames.

Such are the simple headlines of the land situation, but the details of the 'copy' have been shown to be much more complicated.[4] Simplification for the present purpose may result if the account is here confined to three aspects of the evolution of the London Basin which have had most influence on the land situation of the port : the occurrence of glacial Boulder Clay in the northeast ; the diversion of drainage, including the Thames ; and the many minor, but locally important, structures which diversify the general downward sweep of the basin. Continental glaciers creeping down from East Anglia were diverters of drainage, and

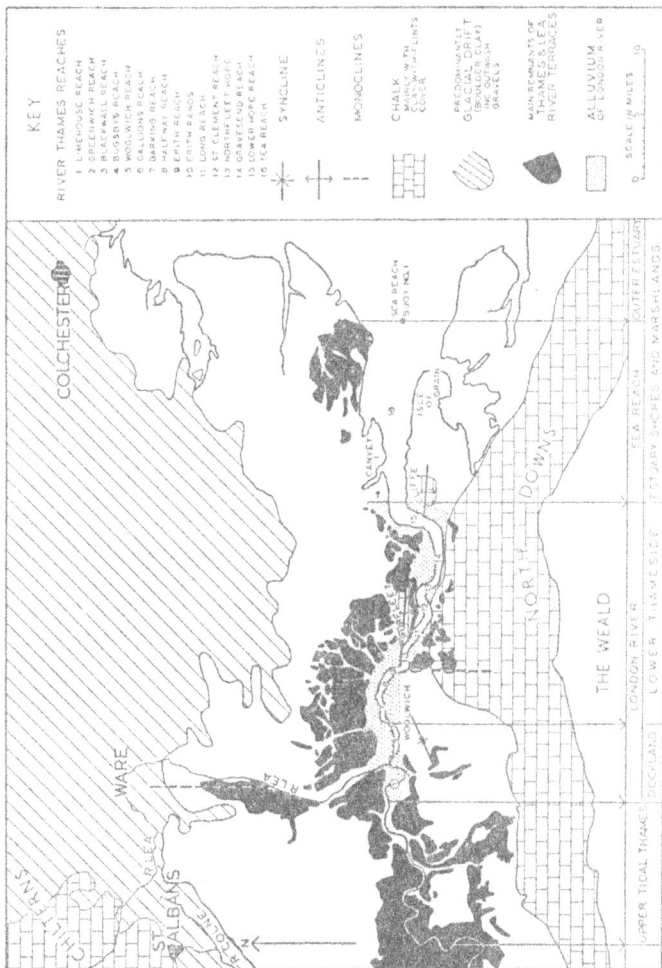

FIG. 1.—Location Diagram showing some Physiographic Aspects of the Port's Situation and Site. The areas left blank consist mainly of Eocene strata, generally London Clay.

the pre-existing rivers, including the Thames, compelled to find new courses, often became embroiled with certain minor structures which otherwise would not have been encountered in that way.

Figure 1 shows these three aspects in generalized form. Only five of the minor structures of the basin have been inserted. There is the north-south monocline, or ruck in the rock structure, down one flank of which the river Lea[5] has shifted sideways to the east. Another north-south monocline through Erith dips to the west and keeps the Chalk higher to the east. This accounts for the Chalk river bluffs at the southward bend of the meanders from Erith to Gravesend; whereas to the west, at Woolwich and at Charlton, west of Woolwich, the river exposes Chalk only at low tide at about the level of O.D. (Newlyn) beneath bluffs cut in Tertiary strata. To the south of Woolwich a syncline, ENE–WSW, has preserved a great thickness of the Tertiary cover overlying the Chalk, and Shooter's Hill rising to 424 feet is composed largely of a remnant of Tertiary London Clay.

The ENE–WSW directions are also exemplified by the Purfleet anticline, which causes an inlier of Chalk to occur and provides the only steep northern slope to the river east of London. This anticline reappears south of Sea Reach at Cliffe.

The deposition of Boulder Clay by Quaternary glaciers was not marked by any moraine-like terminal features. By the time it reached the north-east of the London Basin the ice was nearing the end of its southward journey. The edge of the Glacial Drift is irregular and lobate because material was deposited from a slowly moving mass of ice which was gently adjusting itself to a land of mild relief, and the deposits have since been dissected by the work of post-glacial rivers. Streams nourished by the melting ice deposited outwashed gravel. The pre-glacial rivers, not overrun by the ice, were swollen by meltwater and were often diverted.

This diversion of drainage is an important aspect of the evolution of the London Basin in the present context. If the syncline of the London Basin, pitching towards the North Sea, were to have been symmetrically folded, without subsequent complication, the trunk stream might be expected to flow east-north-east along its central axis. However, such a simple concordance of streams to structure over a wide area is rare. Drainage has to cope with subsequent movements of sea-level and with the irregular distribution of strata deposited in horizontal beds of varying thickness within or above the major structures. The pre-glacial Thames has, in fact, been traced well to the north of the synclinal axis, flowing over an area which has now become the Vale of St. Albans;[6] but east of Ware this early course becomes difficult to determine beneath the glacial deposits. Blocked by these and by the ice itself, the Thames was prevented from follow-ing its course to the north-east via Ware. Finally, the river was diverted to the south never again to pass over the area which became the Vale of St. Albans.[7] This is now drained by two post-glacial tributaries of the Thames: the Colne flows south-west in the Vale; and the Lea first flows east in the Vale and then, follow-ing the monoclinal fold mentioned above, turns south to join the Thames.

The Pleistocene ice-sheet was therefore the chief agent divert-ing the Thames from its pre-glacial course across north Essex to its present position. Although the earlier records of the stages of this diversion in central Essex are difficult to decipher, both the Thames and the Lea have left records of their most recent migra-tions which are important landform features.

If a river becomes incised in its flood-plain, it leaves this upstanding as a terrace along its subsequent course. Terraces are often arranged in sequence if the process of 'down-cutting' is repeated. Now consider the Lower Thames. It is very near the end of its course, and a slight change of sea-level affects it greatly. If the level of the sea should drop relative to the land, the Thames would cut down into its flood-plain. Such down-cutting would pro-ceed progressively upstream from the estuary mouth and would be most marked in the lower course. If the sea-level should rise relative to the land, the newly-formed estuary would be filled up with river-borne debris thus producing another flood-plain. Such a flood-plain might greatly exceed the normal width of the river, because an altering meander pattern would enable its waters to cover a wide swath of territory, widening downstream.

Oscillations of sea-level have taken place since the disappear-ance of the ice from the London Basin. A major cause has been the changes in world climate which have locked up greatly varying amounts of water in expanding or shrinking glaciers. The Lower

Thames has left a terrace record of these oscillations. To repeat the evidence for dating these terraces would cause a digression here.[8] It is generally true to say that the highest terraces are the oldest. East of London the following may be recognized: the Boyn Hill[9] ('100-foot'); the Taplow[9] ('50-foot'); the Flood-plain Terrace; and the flood-plain itself, *i.e.* the alluvium of the river.

These terraces have a much greater extent north of the river. Indeed, east of London the Thames has no northern valley side, only a flight of its terraces which leads up to the Boulder Clay lands of Essex, although the bluffs of the Purfleet anticline are an isolated exception to this arrangement. Although the sea-level fluctuated, the cumulative effect has been a relative downward movement from the time when the Thames laid its Boyn Hill flood-plain. As the river cut down it was able to maintain its course, only slightly influenced by the minor structures across its path. It has just begun to bite at a more serious obstacle which is the dip-foot zone of the Chalk where this emerges on the south side of the main structural basin. The contrast between the north and south shores of London River is therefore great. At Greenwich, Woolwich, Erith, and Gravesend the Thames cuts into formations varying from the Flood-plain Terrace to sedimentary rocks as old as the Chalk, and alluvium is practically absent at the southernmost point of the meanders. The bluff separating the alluvium from the Flood-plain Terrace is generally about 15 feet O.D. On the other hand, north of London River it is this terrace which bounds the alluvium continuously about a mile back from the river until the Purfleet anticline is breached by the river to form a bluff.

The Thames east of London has no valley in the generally accepted sense of that term. It flows on the south side of a very, very shallow staircase with four wide treads and fitfully gnaws at the higher lands of Chalk which would make a resistant barrier to further southward migration at its present level. A final, small, and continuing rise of sea-level has converted the Thames into a river drowned by the sea and opposed twice daily by the tide.

Such are the elements of the structure and drainage evolution relevant to the landward situation of the Port of London. There is little in the immediate hinterland to attract early settlers who needed a large area of relatively light and easily tilled soils in order to support an agricultural population of sufficient density to establish a town. The adjective fertile seems aptly applied to low-lands which by convention are often coloured a fecund green. Yet the lowlands of the London Basin have very varied soils, and few of them are first-class.[10] The Thames itself was flanked by salt-marshes over all the area marked as alluvium on the geological map. Sandy-gravel soils of the Bagshot Plateau, south-west of London, and of the Blackheath Plateau, to the south-east, are natural heathlands, dry and acid. The London Clay lands are wet and heavy, formerly closely covered with oak forest with a dense shrub layer. A loamy soil can develop on the Thames terraces, but their limited extent was emphasized by the fact that they were isolated on three sides by marsh, partitioned by the marshes of sluggish tributaries joining the Thames. Only the spread of Boulder Clay gave rise to a large area of intermediate or loamy soils. Verulamium (St. Albans) and Camulodunum (Colchester) were situated near the edges of this great spread, while Londinium was hemmed in between forest, heath, marsh, and water.[11] One might wonder why Londinium subsequently flourished under the Romans.

The clue lies in its water situation. Consider London as a south-eastern water gateway to this island, and things look very much better. The earliest long-distance traffic to and from Britain must have taken a direction north-west to south-east (and the reverse), from lowland Britain through the London Basin to the earlier developed Roman Empire of continental Europe. Given such a general line of movement, the greatest barriers were the forested clay lands of the Weald, and of the London Clay north of London. These barriers would tend to canalize movement along the North Downs. A centre at Verulamium might focus the routes from the north-east, north-west, and the west, and use the Roman road of Watling Street along the North Downs to reach a Channel port. If this was the best land route for the Romans, a compromise between directness and ease, the water route to London makes only a slight angle with it. No doubt this route entails a detour around the North Foreland of Kent, but the Romans certainly found it useful when transporting goods to and from Britain because, although they constructed excellent roads, their wheeled traffic was rudimentary. Both routes depend on long-distance relations across water with the continent, and the usefulness of London's water situation diminishes if these are broken.

The evidence for this reasoning is the strikingly dissimilar attitudes of the Roman administrators and the Saxon settlers to the situation of London. The Romans, spreading their reach of empire from the continent of Europe, soon recognized the importance of the water situation of London for a nodal base in the network of communications across their organized British state. They even appear to have founded the settlement. This central organization of the Romans was not matched by the Anglo-Saxons who, in contrast, brought into being an assemblage of states, all on a much lower technological level. The Anglo-Saxons were agriculturists and at first only interested in the land, with few commercial links with the mainland of Europe. Entering by the Chelmer and Blackwater estuaries they happily settled on the loamy soils of the Boulder Clay lands which spread down to near the coast in north-east Essex.[12] Although they also sailed up the Thames, they did so only on their entry and literally by-passed sixth century London. To borrow Sir Mortimer Wheeler's graphic phrase, London at that time 'can have mattered little to anyone save to a few decivilized sub-Roman Londoners'.[13] The entrance phase of Saxon settlement, marked by early Saxon burial grounds, reveals no occupance of a site near London.[14]

During the Middle Ages the Roman roads all over Europe deteriorated, whereas water transport developed steadily for its routes needed no upkeep. When long distance routes became re-established between this country and the rest of Europe, the importance of the land and water routes to London was reversed. The Thames dominated and Watling Street now played the subservient role. This has continued until today.

In the London Basin the significance of land situations declined when compared with water situations, and London gained at the expense of towns with poorer water communications. Verulamium and Camulodunum were able to compete with the early Londinium, encircled by forest and heath ; but St. Albans on the Ver and Colchester on the Essex Colne are no match for London on the Thames.

SITE

The local physical features which characterized the land site of the earliest London have been discussed by various authors.[15] Across the river from the twin defensible hills of London, formed from part of the Taplow Terrace cut in two by the Walbrook, there is a gravel tongue of the Flood-plain Terrace. This gave an opportunity for a causeway to approach the river at Southwark, so that the extent of the marshes was greatly reduced.

For terraces thus to approach opposite one another on the banks of a meandering river is unusual. The same process which causes a terrace to be undercut (and so be close to the river) on the outside bend of a meander, also causes alluvium to be deposited on the inner bend. On the inside of the meanders of London River the alluvium is generally over one and a half miles wide. This alluvium is the flood-plain of the river (*see* Figure 1) which would be covered by the highest tides were it not for the river embankments. It is a blue-grey marsh clay interstratified with beds of peat.

The Thames was a barrier not because of its width, but because of the instability of its flanking marshes. Moreover, it must be remembered that since the river is close to its journey's end, the slope to its flood-plain is very slight, both parallel to the river and at right-angles to it. Accordingly, before embanking, any variation of the tide over the marshes would have a magnified lateral variation making it very difficult to establish a permanent embarkation point for a crossing. Most authorities agree that the Southwark site was the lowest place downstream where the Romans could conveniently cross the river. Such a conclusion is, however, not arrived at only by a consideration of the advantages of this site but also by a recognition of the disadvantages of other riparian sites both upstream and downstream.

Examination of present conditions off Southwark does not help, because the tidal range confronting the Romans was considerably less than that operating today.[16] Embankments along the river have canalized the flow, increasing its velocity and causing the tidal limit to migrate upstream; dredging has deepened the river; the alluvium has shrunk after being drained; and there has been a gradual rise of sea-level.

Whether London began in pre-Roman times or as a Romano-British settlement, perhaps the principal function of its land site was to guard a crossing place. As has been shown, with the growth of continental connections, which Roman conquest naturally entailed, the Thames became a trade highway because of its situation. The water site of the terminal transhipment point of this route need not have coincided with the crossing place. Yet two converging tendencies may be noted. At the outset, the Romans undoubtedly founded their central administration at Camulodunum, the capital which Cunobelin, 'King of the Britons', founded in A.D. 5. This necessitated a crossing place as far downstream as possible in order to avoid a long detour via Watling Street, which made for the former capital at Verulamium and is believed to have crossed the river by a ford near the present Westminster. Secondly, for reasons set forth below, the ports of north-western Europe on drowned estuaries were anciently sited as far upstream as possible. These two land and water desiderata : one urging a site as far downstream as possible, when the river is regarded as a barrier ; the other pressing for a site near tidal limits, when the river is regarded as a highway, may well both have been best achieved at the site of London.

The general reasons for the choice of a port site near tidal limits in an estuary may now be set out. Water transport is still the cheapest method of transporting goods in bulk. In early days it was the cheapest method of transport absolutely and often the most convenient. Therefore, it was not abandoned until a point as far inland as possible was reached in order that this should be a distribution point as central as possible. The further inland that ships could penetrate, the further away they were from the navigational dangers of the estuary and the marauders of the open sea when performing the delicate operations of unloading and loading. The tide furnishes a free motive power for ships up and down the estuary. Small river craft voyaging upstream and up tributary waterways would naturally prefer to transfer goods to and from sea-going vessels at a point where the river was the least affected by the vagaries of the tide and as calm as possible. Goods might be transferred to and from ships by wheeled vehicles ; and these vehicles dependent on roads would be equally dependent on bridges which could only be built some distance upstream.

Most of these factors certainly operated in Roman times, suggesting that London fulfilled a port function almost from its foundation. Yet further discussion of the Roman port need not be pursued. Just as the contrasting reactions of the Romans and Saxons illustrated the advantages of the situation, so a study of the Roman reaction alone reveals the advantages of the site for a port and bridgehead. Though it is clear that Londinium was developed as the chief port of Roman Britain, Sir Halford Mackinder surmised that its original *raison d'être* was as the port for Verulamium only.[17] Such dissent is not important, and no shadow is cast across the story of the evolution of the port. When in 410, with the rescript of the Emperor Honorius, the Romans began to leave Britain to its fate, communications with continental Europe became weaker and finally disappeared. This decline was matched by the decline of London; there was a complete interruption of the port function. Then came a slow revival towards the end of the sixth century under the East Saxons, when they were not being harried by the Danes.

An important siting factor must now be considered. If the coincidence of crossing place and transhipment terminal (*i.e.* land site and water site) under the Romans may be deduced on general grounds, in late Saxon times one construction alone would be enough to ensure it—a bridge. Whether or not the Romans built a bridge is not known for certain, but during Saxon times there is no doubt that a timber bridge crossed the river. In such a primitive construction the spans would be very narrow so that vessels of a seaworthy size could only sail upstream of it with difficulty. Separation of river and sea traffic on each side of the bridge would naturally lead to the process of transhipment being performed close by. This tendency would become more marked with the construction of a more permanent narrow-arched stone bridge. The bridge served the Saxon settlement; the settlement protected the bridge. Then, as long-distance water communications were allowed to develop, the excellence of the water situation caused a port function to be carried out close to the site of the bridge. This chapter has been concerned with building up to this chain of reactions which in turn lies below the true, but bare statement: the Thames made London.

Such a stone bridge did in fact for a long time confine the

interplay of these factors close to the Southwark crossing. The foundations of Old London Bridge, which was begun in 1176 and finished in 1209, though many times repaired, did not finally crumble away until 1832. At first it had no less than twenty arches, only thirty feet from one another; and even though equipped with a drawbridge, it soon restricted shipping movements upstream. It is now appropriate to consider some of the main features of the port's development within the life span of this bridge.

## REFERENCES

1. A general systematic study of ports has already appeared in this series. F. W. Morgan, *Ports and Harbours*. (Hutchinson's University Series, 1952.)

2. Reproduced by permission from H. M. Mayer *et al.*, 'Urban Geography', *American Geography, Inventory and Prospect*, edited by P. E. James and C. F. Jones (Syracuse University Press, 1954), Chapter 6, 149.

3. A. E. Smailes, *The Geography of Towns* (Hutchinson's University Series, 1953), 41–2.

4. S. W. Wooldridge and D. L. Linton, *Structure, Surface and Drainage in South-east England* (Philip, 1955), especially Chapters VIII, IX, and X.

5. This more usual spelling is adopted throughout, but the official title of the conservators of this river is the Lee Conservancy Catchment Board.

6. S. W. Wooldridge and D. L. Linton, *loc. cit.*

7. *Ibid.*, and S. W. Wooldridge and G. E. Hutchings, *London's Countryside* (Methuen, 1957), Figure 15.

8. W. B. R. King and K. P. Oakley, 'The Pleistocene Succession in the Lower Part of the Thames Valley', *Proceedings of the Prehistoric Society*, 2 (1936), 52–76.

9. These names derive from the upstream continuation of the terraces in the Middle Thames area where they were first named by H.M. Geological Survey.

10. S. W. Wooldridge, *The Geographer as Scientist* (Nelson, 1956), Figure 24.

11. *Ibid.*, 193–4, and Figure 29.

12. *Ibid.*, 179–83.

13. R. E. M. [now Sir Mortimer] Wheeler, 'Introduction', *Report of the Royal Commission on Historical Monuments*, 3, *Roman London* (1928), 67.

14. S. W. Wooldridge, *The Geographer as Scientist, op. cit.*, Chapter 12, Figure 25.

15. Notably H. Belloc (1912), C. E. N. Bromehead (1922), V. Cornish (1923), W. Page (1923), H. Ormsby (1924), R. E. M. [now Sir Mortimer] Wheeler (1928), *vide supra*, and L. R. Jones (1931). For full details see alphabetical list of references.

16. T. E. Longfield, *The Subsidence of London*. Paper read to the British Association for the Advancement of Science, York, 1932 (Professional Papers, New Series No. 14, H.M.S.O., 1932), 4.

17. At a speech to the Geographical Association in 1922.

# CHAPTER II

# THE DEVELOPMENT OF THE PORT, 1176–1799

THE physical situation and site of the port could be discussed as if they had scarcely changed throughout history. In the human or, more narrowly, the economic geography of the Port of London the time element must be considered. A history of the port has long since been written by an observer uniquely placed because of his experience at a critical period of the port's development.[1] Here no attempt is made to paraphrase this history. Instead, two word pictures will be reproduced: one shows the port as it appeared to an observer at the beginning of the seventeenth century; and the other is based on a Parliamentary Report at the end of the eighteenth century. In addition, certain events will be mentioned which have cast the longest shadows down the path of the port's development.

In the first chapter, the building of a quasi-permanent stone bridge was seen to have been an important factor in promoting a stable nucleus for a port on the banks of the Thames. 1176, the year of the commencement of Old London Bridge, serves therefore as a useful point of departure.

## QUEENHITHE AND BILLINGSGATE

Under the Saxon kings two hithes, or artificial inlets with wooden piles to prevent the sides slipping in, had been created on the north bank, on each side of the Southwark crossing. The history of these, according to John Stow,[2] may be briefly treated.

Queenhithe had occurred first as 'Ætheredys Hythe' in a charter of Alfred in 899. This landing place appears to have been in the King's possession, and there is definite evidence that in the twelfth century Henry I gave it to his Queen, Matilda; hence the name. In a charter of Henry II it is described as '*Ripa Reginae que appellatur Atheres hithe*'. In 1224 Henry III commanded the Constable of the Tower of London to arrest the ships of the Cinque Ports on the Thames and compel them to bring their corn only to Queenhithe. Moreover, in 1226 he further commanded the Constable to confiscate all fish which was not sold at Queenhithe. Towards the middle of the century foreign ships laden with fish arrived at Billingsgate contrary to the King's order. This came to the notice of the Bailiffs of Queenhithe, and it was ordered that if any foreign ship laden with fish landed at a place other than Queenhithe, it should be fined forty shillings, though ships belonging to citizens of London could arrive where their owners decided.

By 1463 the market at Queenhithe was found to be hindered by the slackness in raising the drawbridge within London Bridge. It was therefore ordered that all vessels making for the port with food should follow this arrangement: if the vessels arrived one at a time, they must unload and make sale at Queenhithe; but if two vessels arrived, one should go to Queenhithe, the other to Billingsgate; and if three, two of them should go to Queenhithe, the third to Billingsgate, so that Queenhithe should always have more. If the vessel was so heavily laden that it could not arrive at these hithes, its cargo was to be conveyed by lighters. Queenhithe had a warehouse for corn built in 1554 and enlarged in 1565 by the Mayor and City of London, to whom it had been farmed by the King in 1245. Nevertheless, the orders quoted above prove that it still continued to be favoured by the King to the detriment of Billingsgate.

This latter hithe, downstream of London Bridge, seems also to have been quite ancient, and the origin of the name is obscure. Stow quite sensibly suggests that it was named after a Beling or Biling, since many of the wharves were named after former owners. Though not the recipient of royal favours like Queenhithe, London Bridge did not blockade its water approach, so that as Queenhithe declined, Billingsgate prospered. By 1603 it had developed into the chief larder door for the entry of London's imported food.

'Queen-hithe being above bridge, near to the Steelyard [Hanseatic] Wharf, was probably the most convenient "hythe" or port for foreign merchants; whilst Billingsgate and its vicinity, the ancient seat of trade below the bridge, was more especially the seat of the domestic business. We can understand from this, that the restoration of the trade to Billingsgate was a concession to the native London merchants.'[3]

The decline of Queenhithe certainly appears to be contemporaneous with the decline of the influence of foreign merchants during the second half of the sixteenth century.

### FOREIGN MERCHANTS AND EVENTS IN THE SIXTEENTH CENTURY

In the early history of London's commerce important roles were played by foreign merchants.[4] The counterpart of the Lombards in banking were the Hansards in shipping. One of the reasons why London was able to re-enter continental trade after its early Saxon eclipse was the fact that the merchants of Cologne, of the western group of the Hanseatic League, had a depot and privileges in London as early as the twelfth century. For a time they were the chief merchants of the port, although the English wool merchants became the first to break their monopoly by 1350.[5] Gradually, alien traders, of which the Hansards were the chief, found that English merchants were taking over their trade. Probably, this first occurred because of the expansion of the English cloth industry during the fourteenth century, when English merchants were forced to find new markets for their increased production. Foreign merchants would no doubt be at a disadvantage when their trading privileges came into review alongside those of their English rivals. These became so powerful that they were able to reduce the influence of the Hanseatic traders. Stow puts it laconically:

> 'In the yeare 1551. and the fift of *Edward* the sixt, through complaint of the English marchants, the libertie of the Stilliard [or Hanseatic] Marchants was seised into the kings hands, and so it resteth.'[6]

The German merchants thus lost their exclusive privileges, and later, in 1597, Elizabeth I, encouraged by the growth of English commerce, arbitrarily expelled the Hansards from the port.

Foreign competition was also reduced in the sixteenth century through the destruction of the Spanish Armada, the occupation of the southern Low Countries by Spain, and the sack of Antwerp in

1576 and its capture in 1585. This port was London's chief rival until these disasters.

Two other events in the port's history during the sixteenth century may be mentioned. Royal Dockyards were established at Deptford and Woolwich in 1513.[7] The latter came into being as the building site of Henry VIII's famous *Henri Grace à Dieu*, of 1600 tons, which when launched became the world's largest ship.

More importantly, the reign of Elizabeth I saw a development of overseas trade, not only because of naval victories, but because the Queen was interested in England's aggrandizement rather than in the religious controversies which had been the preoccupation of her predecessors. For example, the Russia, Eastland (or North Sea), Turkey, and East India Companies all received their charters of establishment in the second half of the sixteenth century. In 1558, the first year of Elizabeth's reign, a commission was appointed to establish 'legal quays' where dutiable goods would have to be landed. Previously, the revenue officers had often experienced great difficulty in locating a cargo on which they had to levy duty. Only a few hours' notice could be given of a sailing ship's arrival, and there was no regular berthing system. In London, the Legal Quays selected were all situated on the north bank of the river between the Tower and London Bridge, along a total frontage of 1,464 feet. After their establishment the amount of customs revenue doubled.

## The Port in 1603

A general view of the Port of London at the beginning of the seventeenth century may be gleaned by reading selectively through the pages of Stow's celebrated *Survey of London*, first published in 1598, with a second revised edition in 1603. The main body of Stow's work consists of a tour round the several wards of the City of London, and the following is based on appropriate passages, beginning with a brief verbatim extract which gives an idea of the clear and lively style.

'*Thames* the most famous riuer of this Iland, beginneth a little aboue a village called *Winchcombe* in Oxfordshire, and still increasing passeth first by the university of Oxford, and so with a maruelous quiet course to *London*, and thence breaketh into the French Ocean by maine tides, which twice in 24. howers space doth ebb and flow, more then 60. miles in length, to the great commoditie of Trauellers, by which all kind of Marchandise bee easily conueyed to *London*, the principall store house, and Staple of all commodities within this Realme, . . .'[8]

However, a tributary of the Thames, the river Fleet, had long since lost its value as a place of concourse for shipping. As early as 1306 complaints had been made that whereas at one time it had been of such breadth and depth that ten or twelve ships could sail up to Fleet Bridge, or even Oldbourne (Holborn) Bridge, now (1306) the course was much reduced by debris poured into it especially by tanners, by wharves raised alongside, and by diversion of water to the mills of the Temple in 1200. The river was accordingly improved in 1307 and many times during the fourteenth century but never brought to its former depth and breadth. In 1502 cargoes of fish and fuel were rowed up the river, but, notwithstanding an attempt at cleansing it in 1589, it was in 1603 worse choked than ever before. By this date the Walbrook had already been for some time arched over with brick and built upon so that no casual observer would know of its course.

From near the east bank of the confluence of the river Fleet with the Thames (the present Blackfriars Station) to the Tower of London, or from near the south-west to the south-east corner of the City of London, ran the most important street of the port, named Thames Street appropriately enough. Along both sides of this street and in the area leading down to the north bank of the river were concentrated the buildings which made up the early seventeenth century Port of London.

On the Thames side of this street were a number of wharves. They were often named after their owners, and so the names were liable to change. Let it be supposed that John Stow surveyed the waterfront in the following direct order from west to east, that is from the encumbered estuary of the Fleet to the Tower of London. The figures in the text represent the feature on the location diagram, Figure 2.

West of the Fleet was the poor-house of Bridewell, and the

area within the eastern angle of the Fleet and the Thames was occupied by the establishment of the Black Friars. Adjacent to this on the east was Puddle Wharf (1), apparently so called because horses used to be watered there, and the ground, poached by their trampling, was often covered by puddles. Beyond this was a brewhouse (2), Baynard's Castle (3), and Pauls Wharf (5) hemmed in between a messuage (4) and property belonging to the Earl of Huntingdon (6) and the City of London (7). Broken

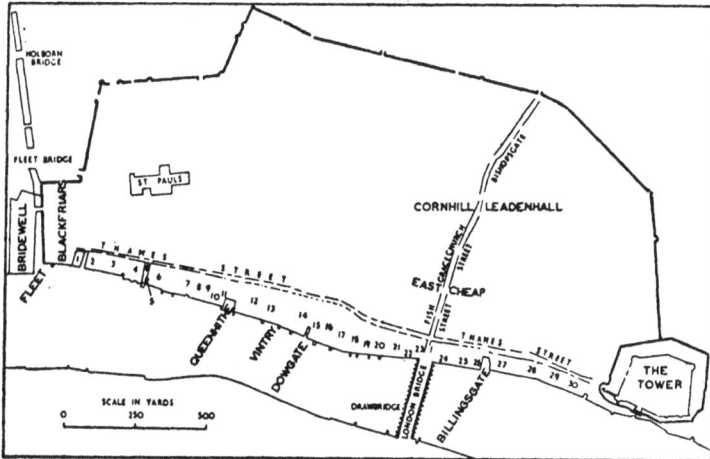

FIG. 2.—The Port of London, 1603.
The key to the thirty riverside frontages is given in the text.

Wharf (8) was a ruin in 1603, succeeded by Brookes Wharf (9), Timber Wharf (10), where timber was landed and stored, and Salt Wharf (11), where salt was landed, measured, and sold.

Between the almost forsaken Queenhithe and the Vintry were the Black Swan Brewery (12) and tenements (13). At the Vintry Wharf merchants of Bordeaux had discharged their wines by cranes from lighters and other vessels until 1299 when they complained of taxes. This was put right by a King's writ, and many large houses were built in Vintry Ward with vaults and cellars for the stowage of wine. The wharf was equipped with three timber cranes in 1603. Before Dowgate, which like Queenhithe had

C

declined greatly, there was another brewhouse (14); and beyond there was a dye house (15), the former depot of the merchants of Cologne (16), Hay Wharf (17), tenements (18), Dyers Hall (19), and more brewhouses (20). Fishmongers Hall (21), with Fish Wharf (22) and Drinkwater Wharf (23), completed the waterfront west of the bridge.

In Thames Street, east and west of the bridge, there were merchants' warehouses, and some of their houses were on the bridge itself. In Fish Street, leading north from the bridge, were fishmongers, and further north, in Gracechurch Street, was a corn market.[9]

Buttolphes Wharf (24), just east of the bridge, was followed by two wharves taking the name of former owners, Lion Key (25) and Sommers Key (26), and then Billingsgate.

By 1603 this was a large inlet for ships arriving there regularly with cargoes of fresh and salt fish, all kinds of fruit, and grain for the City and its immediate hinterland.

Adjacent to Billingsgate, on the east, were Smarts Key (27) and Porters Key (28). Next to the latter there was Wool Wharf and the Custom House (29).

In 1382 John Churchman, a grocer, built a house on Wool Wharf, close to the Tower of London, to serve for the weighing of wools in the Port of London. The King granted that this should be done there during this man's lifetime, and privileges were also given to allow the establishment of balances and weights and a counting house for the Customer and his officials. Such was the origin of Customers Key and the Custom House.

Next to the Customers Key, and last before the Tower, came Galley Key (30), where galleys from Italy and other Mediterranean countries discharged their cargoes, notably wine. It is supposed that merchants dealing with these cargoes procured the ground behind the wharf for the building of their lodgings and storehouses, though by 1603 there had been no such traffic within living memory. The building had either fallen into ruin or had been put to other uses.

A final gleaning from Stow may be added:

'. . . there pertayneth to the Cities of *London*, *Westminster*, and Burrough of *Southwarke*, aboue the number as is supposed

of 2000. Wherryes and other small boats, whereby 3000. poore
men at the least bee set on worke and maintained.'[10].

This is the portrait of the Port of London in 1603. Undoubtedly, the account of the waterfront is not complete, and it
is a pity that the functions of some of the wharves are not more
closely described. However, the great value of the survey is
without question; but before making further comments on the
picture it presents, let the lay-out of a theoretical and simple
general cargo port be considered.

The shore would be artificially built up to ensure a definite
vertical face between land and water. Ships' cargoes would be
dumped on the horizontal 'made ground' beyond the vertical face.
These goods would accumulate because a ship is a much bigger
unit of transport than a land vehicle, and perfect synchronization
of cargo movement is not possible. In any case, some time must
elapse for the sorting of those cargoes not in bulk. So behind the
line of wharves, in an area parallel to the quays, warehouses might
be expected. There would be a point along the waterfront where,
because of centrality, and perhaps for some additional reason,
traffic would be greatest, and from this point a road would lead
to an inland distributing centre. Away from this central spine the
wharves would become progressively less valuable until the
commercial waterfront would be limited by some natural feature
or defence work of the port. Longitudinal communication parallel
to the shore would be necessary because goods would have to be
marshalled for distribution inland and overseas. The outline of
the port would tend to be a semi-circle with the line of wharves
forming the diameter, and the central spine would be a radius at
right-angles to it.

An exact replica of such a theoretical port cannot be expected
to exist at any time. Yet the abstract reasoning does provide a
standard external shape and interior pattern for a port. Such a
yardstick aids the recognition of unusual elements in the lay-out
of the port studied, or if the port be very large, helps to identify
the old nuclear areas. This 'ideal' pattern has been dilated on
here because the picture presented by Stow reproduces many
elements of it.

The chief feature was the line of wharves from the Fleet to

the Tower, with Fish Street and Gracechurch Street as the inland
spine leading from the concentration of traffic at the northern end
of Old London Bridge. The longitudinal street uniting the wharves
and warehouses was Thames Street, where, in addition, about
twenty halls of important guilds and companies were situated.
Cornhill, Leadenhall, and Eastcheap would represent the inland
markets, and there were fishmongers and a corn market, it will be
remembered, in Fish and Gracechurch Streets which led thither.
Of course, there were other markets as well, distributed about the
periphery of the City, which besides being a seaport was also a
domestic collecting and distributing centre for products of its
hinterland. Yet despite its other non-port functions, the City was
girdled by a wall which was virtually semi-circular, asymmetri-
cally distributed about a Fish Street-Gracechurch Street-Bishops-
gate 'radius'.

However, the analogy of the theoretical port read into Stow's
London must not be pushed beyond its usefulness. The line of the
City wall, though probably based on the Roman desire to protect
the twin hills, the river frontage, and the bridgehead, was locally
determined by the line of minor slopes, and it is somewhat of a
coincidence that in 1603 it should have had so few irregularities
that a semi-circular shape can still be recognized.[11] London is
of course much more than a port; but consider the functions of
London which are at some remove from the port function and
recall where they are: national administration, justice, social
centres (shops, theatres, hotels, parks, etc.), communication
termini, modern light and heavy industries, newspapers, and
residential areas. Almost all are situated outside that 'semi-circle'
of the City. When the City of London, east of the Fleet, comprised
the whole built-up area, the port function of London was
relatively more dominant than it is today.

In 1603 the port's activities were undoubtedly concentrated
between Thames Street and the river, yet the bridge had caused a
differentiation. Queenhithe and Dowgate had both declined in
relation to Billingsgate, and Stow mentions only a few wharves
west of the bridge, one of which had been allowed to fall into ruin.
Such hithes and wharves were no doubt kept in business by some
of the 2,000 lighters which could navigate London Bridge and
circumvent the bottleneck of its drawbridge. It is surely sig-

nificant that such specialized wharves as Stow mentions should all be west of the bridge, with the exception of Wool Wharf. This implies that cargoes were landed east of the bridge, at the Legal Quays, because they were dutiable; but many of the products passing upstream of the bridge, especially those in lighters, had already been sorted for the convenience of their specialized landing places. The merchants of Bordeaux, for instance, at their establishment in the Vintry, 'craned their wines out of Lighters'. Such auxiliary craft enabled land distribution and collection to take place along a line of quays. This requirement and the obstruction of the bridge are the chief factors in the early use of large numbers of lighters in the Port of London, a feature which has subsequently continued to distinguish it.

The cramping effect of the bridge may be further seen in the fact that all the Legal Quays were downstream of it, and that upstream of it houses, including Baynard's Castle, were permitted to have frontages on the river. Moreover, as late as 1282, Edward I allowed the Archbishop of Canterbury to enlarge Blackfriars Church; and Bridewell, the Kings' house opposite to the Black Friars across the estuary of the Fleet, was given to the citizens of London as a workhouse for the poor as late as 1553. The Kings knew what they were doing. What might appear to have been an economically useful confluence of tributary and river was blockaded by the bridge downstream, and so the Fleet was allowed to be choked by debris from the land and its banks given over to non-port uses. Furthermore, many brewers and dyers, who would need waterside sites, were able to establish themselves on the relatively slack waterfront upstream of the bridge.

Up to this time few port functions are to be discovered on the south bank of the river. Congestion on the north side had not yet reached a point where an overflow was demanded. Only with the greatest reluctance would the merchants migrate from the north bank. A port depends on intimate connection with its business houses, and before telegraphy this entailed physical proximity.

The emergence of specialized landing places may be re-emphasized. The area near Billingsgate was already the home of the fish trade, though of many other trades as well. Wool, wine, timber, salt, and hay all had their appropriate quays.

Such is the general picture of the port at the beginning of the seventeenth century. Now let the picture of the port nearly two hundred years later be boldly placed against this.[12]

THE PORT IN 1796

The title of the great report of 1796[13] indicates that there was then something seriously amiss in the Port of London. Fortunately, the opening sections of this document are a valuable description of the port at that time, and appropriate passages form the basis of the account reproduced here.

Trade statistics for the eighteenth century were provided by the Inspector General of Customs.

TABLE I

*Port of London: Imports and Exports, 1700–1794*[14]

| Year | | | Value of Imports | Value of Exports |
|------|---|---|------------------|------------------|
| | | | (Million Pounds) | |
| 1700 ... | ... | ... | 4·88 (80 per cent) | 5·39 (74 per cent) |
| 1720 ... | ... | ... | 4·96 | 5·00 |
| 1750 ... | ... | ... | 5·54 (71 per cent) | 8·41 (66 per cent) |
| 1770 ... | ... | ... | 8·89 | 9·27 |
| 1790 ... | ... | ... | 12·28 (70·5 per cent) | 10·71 (56 per cent) |
| 1794 ... | ... | ... | 14·86 | 16·58 |

(Figures in brackets are the percentage total trade of the country. About half the exports were foreign goods transhipped.)

Comparison of annual trade returns by value over a long period is often vitiated by the decrease in the value of money. However, the Inspector General of Customs took care to explain in evidence that an estimate was made of the value of foreign goods imported in 1696 and that this was used as a basis for the valuation of goods in customs documents in the hundred years up to the 1796 report. The figures may therefore be compared with some confidence.

From 1700 to 1770 the trade of the Port of London had nearly doubled, and in the quarter of a century from 1770 to 1794 the increase appeared equal to the whole progressive course of commerce in the seventy years before.

This increase of trade was matched by an increase of shipping.

TABLE II

*Coastwise Vessels using the Port of London,*
*Entered inwards, 1700, 1750, and 1795[15]*

| Year | | | | Number | Average Tonnage per Vessel |
|------|---|---|---|--------|---------------------------|
| 1700 ... | ... | ... | ... | 5,562 | 50 |
| 1750 ... | ... | ... | ... | 6,396 | 80 |
| 1795 ... | ... | ... | ... | 11,964 | 100 |

TABLE III

*Number of Ships using the Port of London,*
*Entered inwards from Foreign Ports, 1702, 1751, and 1795[16]*

| Year | | British | Foreign | Average Tonnage per Vessel |
|------|---|---------|---------|---------------------------|
| 1702 ... | ... | 839 | 496 | 118 |
| 1751 ... | ... | 1,498 | 184 | 139 |
| 1795 ... | ... | 1,841 | 991 | 205 |

Not only was the number of vessels doubled during the course of the century, but the average tonnage of vessels was likewise doubled, so that the total tonnage of vessels using the port was quadrupled.

The number of ships for which there was adequate room at mooring tiers and mooring chains from London Bridge to Deptford was estimated to be 613;[17] the number of vessels frequently to be found there was nearly 900, exclusive of craft;[18] occasionally as many as 1,400 sail lay in the river at one time. The result was that ships were often crowded into very shallow water and at low tide were grounded and received damage, sometimes even lost. The difficulties of mooring further downstream were pointed out: there was the disadvantage of increased distance from the quays and warehouses; there was an increased hazard for the craft necessary to convey the cargoes because of the length and difficulty of the navigation; and, resulting from this, there was an increased risk of plunder. For these reasons ships of all sizes would have preferred to come up to the Pool if there had been sufficient room and depth of water.

The problems of congestion were aggravated by the seasonal

arrival of shipping in the West Indian and timber trades; the convoy system operating in times of war; and the increase, during the seventeenth century, of the collier fleet supplying the rapidly growing London with domestic fuel. The tonnage of coal landed annually in London increased from 380,000 in 1726–32 to about 720,000 in 1796, brought by over 4,000 colliers.[19] Often 90 of these colliers would be discharging at one time in the Pool, and as they each loaded into a dozen barges, about 1,100 craft would be laden with coal at one time. Every other ship of the 400-strong timber fleet arrived with a cargo of logs, and when these were rafted in the river they occupied ten times the space of the ship.[20]

'A further complaint made, is, of neglect and bad practices respecting the ships when at their stations; and which occasion delay in the delivery of their cargoes, and give opening to plunder and to frauds on the revenue. . . . This was due to . . . the beginning to unload ships when the cargo is but partially entered . . . inattention of masters and mates quitting their ships before discharge of their cargoes, and leaving the care of them to a description of persons called Lumpers; to permitting these, and other persons on board the ships, to wear loose trowsers and dresses suited to the secreting goods, . . . the plunderage and smuggling is generally carried on with the connivance of the Revenue officers stationed in the ship, and who come on board perfectly prepared with instruments, and bladders to draw off and secure their share of the plunder; and that he [the witness] has generally understood from these officers, that their pay was inadequate, and that they could not subsist without (what they were pleased to term) perquisites.'[21]

Ships did not always moor at stations suited to their draught, often occupying stations which could accommodate much bigger ships. In addition, ships did not moor in any way according to either their dimensions or cargoes.

Further congestion was due to the number of craft (cutters, barges, and punts) from 20–70 tons, of which the total number in service at any one time was 3,500. A pilot of Trinity House stated that the river was so filled up with shipping that a boat could not pass, that ships often ran foul of each other, and that he himself had been delayed for seven days from moving up river from Deptford.

There was 'A great and general complaint . . . of inattention to a proper conservation of the depth of the river'. Sailing ships experienced difficulty in rounding the Isle of Dogs because of the eddies and shoals in the river and the changes of wind required.

All these complaints issue from one outstanding and almost incredible fact which emerges in a comparison of the port in 1603 and 1796. Despite the interval of nearly 200 years and the enormous increase of trade, the 1,419 feet[22] of the Legal Quays, only 40 feet wide, were still the nucleus of the port. All craft with dutiable goods had to work within tidal distance of them.

Certainly, the nature of the ancillary accommodation had changed. The Great Fire of 1666 had destroyed most of the old warehouses. Indeed, the congested port area was one of the causes of the rapid spread of the fire, because it started in Pudding Lane, a crowded thoroughfare which led back from the teeming waterfront, just east of Fish Street.

Beginning with an Act in 1663, several Sufferance Wharves were permitted to extend the inadequate and crowded quay frontage. Because of the overwhelming congestion at the Legal Quays even in the seventeenth century, the Commissioners of Customs had allowed certain goods to be landed at other quays through special sufferance. The extent of these Sufferance Wharves, as they came to be called, is shown in 1789 (Figure 3). This diagram when compared with that of the port in 1603 illustrates the fact that the centre of gravity of the port while still balanced on the line of Legal Quays, was now definitely downstream of London Bridge.

The Sufferance Wharves added about 3,700 feet of quay frontage, but this made London's total quay length still little more than that of Bristol. Only the lower quality of foreign merchandize and goods in bulk (like coal, stone, timber, and grain) were landed at these wharves because the sufferance was of a rather precarious nature ; and owners of such premises were not therefore encouraged to sink capital into the construction of new warehouses. Nevertheless, they dealt with practically all the coastal trade, where no customs duty was levied. Through lack of an assured trade, there were no markets near the Sufferance Wharves. Often their landing charges were even higher than at the Legal Quays. Revenue officers certainly charged more, because they always claimed 'extra' fees when operating elsewhere than at the Legal Quays. However, the greatest disadvantage of the Sufferance Wharves was no doubt their distance from established commercial houses and markets.

What of the Legal Quays themselves? The chaos there must

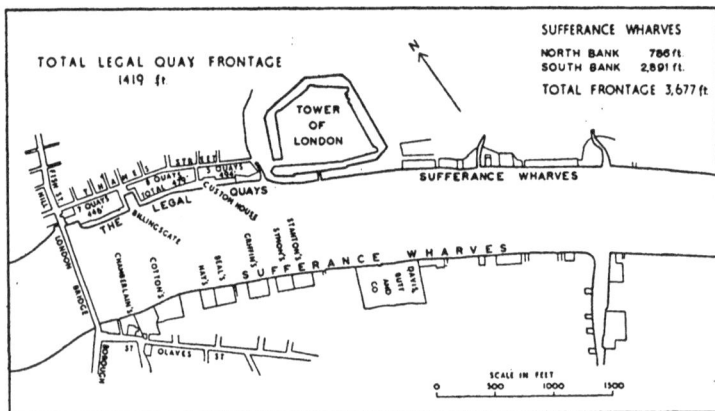

FIG. 3.—The Port of London, 1789.
Based on a plan in Appendix (Uu) 2 of the *Report* (1796), *op. cit.*

have been prodigious. The export and import trades were huddled together to their mutual disadvantage. Amid the general press of transhipment, markets were held for spirits, oils, fruit, and other merchandise. The Revenue officers were too few and badly regulated. Barges were frequently delayed from discharging for as long as six weeks. Seizures of goods were often made because they could not be landed within the time prescribed by law. These time limits were not unduly restrictive: for example, wines had to be unloaded within twenty-one days, and rums and coffee within thirty days; but ships often took two or three months to unload. The wharfingers at the Legal Quays generally required that goods landed at their quays should be stored in their warehouses. Yet, to take an example from the sugar trade, these had capacity for only 32,000 hogsheads of sugar. The annual import of sugar was 100,000-120,000 hogsheads, and this arrived within three months of the year. Even if dispensation were given, the Sufferance Wharves could only store 60,000 hogsheads at the maximum, provided that they were free of their usual general cargo. The result was that hogsheads of sugar were often piled as much as eight high on the Legal Quays, with but little protection from the weather.

Behind the Legal Quays no less than ten streets led inland at right angles to Thames Street; all were narrow and crowded and added to the jam of traffic about the quays themselves. The entire operation of transferring cargo was riddled with the risk of plunder, a hazard which was intensified at every bottle-neck and delay.

P. Colquhoun (1800), the founder of the Thames Marine Police in 1798, estimated that a quarter of the 36,000 men engaged in port work were delinquent.[23] To these must be added 1,200 'professionals': river pirates, night plunderers (of barges), 'light horsemen' (night plunderers of ships), receivers, and mudlarks.[24] Their depredations amounted to 0.84% of the total trade of the port. Nearly half this enormous loss, amounting to about £230,000 annually, was borne by the West India merchants. This was equivalent to 2% of the West India trade, and the following table helps to explain why this was so.

TABLE IV

*Percentage of Total Imports to London by Value, 1797*[25]

| Origin | | | | | Thousand Tons |
|---|---|---|---|---|---|
| East Indies | ... | ... | ... | ... 21 | 41 |
| West Indies | ... | ... | ... | ... 23 | 101 |
| North America | | ... | ... | ... 5 | — |
| North-west and Central Europe | | | ... | 14 | — |
| Mediterranean Europe | | ... | ... | 5 | — |
| Russia | ... | ... | ... | ... 5 | — |
| Africa | ... | ... | ... | ... 3 | — |
| Coastal Trade ... | ... | ... | ... | 25 | 1,254 |

(Colliers account for 50% of coastal tonnage)

From this it emerges that the traffic originating from the East and West Indies and the coastal trade accounted for practically three-quarters of the imports of the port (by value). Furthermore, it can be seen that the East and West India cargoes were incomparably more valuable per unit of weight.

Now the East India trade was well protected. Many of the Indiamen discharged in Blackwall Reach, where the East India Dock is situated today, and the goods were conveyed under armed guard by the well-disciplined employees of the company. The great Cutler Street warehouses, built by the East India Company, are a massive barrack-like structure, well away from the turbulent riverside (*see* front endpaper).

The West India trade was organized in no such manner. The merchants engaged in it relied on the warehouses of the Legal Quays, and were of course thoroughly alive to their disadvantages. They petitioned the City Court of Aldermen in 1674, and Parliament in 1705 and 1763. Each time the question came up only to be shelved; and the merchants were for a long time too divided amongst themselves to agree on plans for building new alternative installations.

The matter was allowed to drift even though the average annual import of sugar had trebled during the eighteenth century. It was this fact which enabled London to maintain its 70% share of the country's rapidly expanding trade in the half century from 1750 to 1800.

This vast increase in the port's trade caused the seething mass of inefficiency, delay, and plunder to rise up to a boiling point. When William Vaughan, a director of the Royal Exchange Assurance, became the spokesman for the West India Merchants, the crisis in the port had merely to be expounded for it to be obvious that something had to be done. The solution was undoubtedly the excavation of wet docks, but opponents had to be propitiated and plans concerted. This took six years.

### THE ADVANTAGES OF WET DOCKS ON THE THAMES

Before proceeding with a summary of the important discussions which took place between 1793 and 1799, it is perhaps useful to consider the advantages that wet docks possess. Where the tidal range is more than fifteen feet (as it is on the Thames as far upstream as London Bridge), wet docks are generally less costly than tidal basins. In the latter case there is the additional capital cost of constructing stronger quay walls to withstand variations in pressure between the high and low tides. Moreover, the saving on lock gates and machinery would be more than offset by the capital cost of the greater depth required for the basin and its foundations, *given such a range*. The task of dredging is infinitely greater in a tidal basin compared with an enclosed dock.

It is true that entrance locks are dangerous bottle-necks for traffic. The larger vessels can only use them during the hours of higher tide levels. Yet again other disadvantages of tidal berths weigh heavier. A contemporary illustration of these disadvantages is provided by the present Cargo Jetty, in Gravesend Reach, which forms part of the Tilbury Docks system (*see* back endpaper). This magnificently constructed jetty has thirty feet of water at low tide. Yet it is not often used by vessels. Although the tide runs strongly and keeps the berth clean, saving dredging costs, it results in mooring difficulties. As a vessel rises and falls with the tide constant attention must be given to prevent sheering and ranging, and the main engines must be kept at the ready. Sea watches need to be maintained on board, and, consequently, none of the crew can be sent on leave. No engine overhauls or minor maintenance refitting can be undertaken.[26]

In the early days the vast areas of land needed for docks could be acquired very cheaply away from the river frontage. With the exception of the sites of the London and St. Katharine Docks, few of the marsh areas chosen for dock excavation were used for anything but pasture. With large acreages of cheap land available, docks and warehouses could be built as one unit, surrounded, if necessary, by a defensive wall. In this way warehouse accommodation was increased at the same time as smuggling and plunder were put down, the revenue safeguarded, and, most importantly, from which all the rest depended, congestion of traffic on the river was lessened.

William Vaughan (1793) in an historic tract was the first to suggest definite sites for wet docks to relieve the congestion on the river. Such docks were of course no novelty, and Vaughan was able to point to successful examples, notably at Liverpool and Le Havre.

Moreover, as early as 1696 the royal assent had been given for the construction of the Howland Wet Dock, 1,070 feet by 500 feet, with a 17-foot depth. This was on the site of the present Greenland Dock of the Surrey Commercial Docks. At first, this dock was used merely for repair and refitting; 120 sailing ships could be accommodated for refit. Early engravings show it surrounded by trees which acted as wind-breaks, but there were no warehouses. The dock was not originally intended for commerce since it was too far downstream. Its owners hoped to get the overflow of repair work from the nearby Royal Dockyard at Deptford. In 1763 the dock was renamed the Greenland Dock, being a base for whalers in Arctic waters.

Another small dock, Brunswick Dock, was a private venture of a Mr. Perry and was situated just south of the present East India Import Dock. It had developed from what was probably the first dock on Thameside, constructed about 1660, and was used by ships of the East India Company principally as a masting and fitting out dock. The Indiamen unloaded their cargoes in the river, in Blackwall Reach, or even partially in Long Reach if they were too heavily laden to navigate the upper reaches of the river in safety.

Though both these docks were later absorbed into larger dock systems, in the 1790's they were merely 'parking places' for ships and not commercial ventures. General cargoes could not be landed at either because there were no warehouses or customs facilities. Nevertheless, they had given an example of the convenience and safety of wet docks. As early as 1703 it had been observed that the ships in the Howland Dock had escaped the havoc which had been wreaked by a great storm on shipping caught in the river.

Apart from the general advantages of wet docks for a port with a pronounced tidal range, there were certain additional advantages which operated in the 1790's. These were closely related to the costs of the necessary operations which obtained at that time. The chief items in the expense account of a ship discharging in the river were the high costs of unloading, lighterage, and warehouse rent. It is difficult to distinguish the general advantages of wet docks from the special advantages obtaining in 1796, but their combined effect is fortunately well illustrated by the following table.

TABLE V

*Comparison of Expenses for a Ship of 260 tons, from the West Indies, discharging in Proposed London Dock, Wapping and in the River Thames, 1796*[27]

|  | Docks | | | River | | |
|---|---|---|---|---|---|---|
| Pilotage from the Downs to the River ... ... | The same | | | | | |
| Ship delivered in (days) ... ... ... ... | 14 | | | 30 | | |
|  | £ | s. | d. | £ | s. | d. |
| Maintenance of {3 Customs / 2 Excise} Officers at 1s. per day | 3 | 10 | 0 | 7 | 10 | 0 |
| Wages and Maintenance of Watchmen until the Cargo is landed ... ... ... ... | 2 | 2 | 0 | 10 | 10 | 0 |
| Boat attending the Ship and Maintenance of Man | 2 | 0 | 0 | 7 | 0 | 0 |
| Expenses of Delivery of Cargo under Crane in Dock ... ... ... ... ... | 10 | 0 | 0 | — | — | — |
| Expenses of Delivery of Cargo into Lighters ... | — | — | — | 25 | 0 | 0 |
| Wear and Tear of cables lying at anchor, at least | — | — | — | 8 | 0 | 0 |
| Ship lying at Chains for 5 weeks (10s. per week) | — | — | — | 2 | 10 | 0 |
| Warehouse Rent on 350 hogsheads of sugar paid to the Wharfinger, from Ship's Report until the Cargo is landed; 3 weeks at 3d. per hogshead per week ... ... ... ... | — | — | — | 13 | 2 | 6 |
| Lighterage on 350 hogsheads of sugar at 1s. 3d. / 100 puncheons of rum at 1s. } | — | — | — | 26 | 17 | 6 |
| Dock Dues ... ... ... ... ... ... | 22 | 15 | 0 | — | — | — |
| Total expenses in docks and river ... | £40 | 7 | 0 | £100 | 10 | 0 |
| Balance in Favour of Docks ... ... | £60 | 3 | 0 | | | |

## THE GREAT DEBATE, 1793–1799

When Vaughan wrote in 1793 he was convinced that wet docks were necessary to the port, and his problem was to suggest possible sites for their excavation. With remarkable prescience, he recommended sites at St. Katharines, Hermitage, Wapping, Isle of Dogs, and extensions at the Brunswick and Greenland Docks. All these recommendations became fact within thirty-five years of his writing, and within his lifetime.

Of the sites he mentioned, Vaughan believed that Wapping would be the most advantageous, since it was the closest to the City with the exception of St. Katharines, but entailed destruction of less property to the acre than that more restricted site. At first, the London merchants were content to let him speak for them. Later, during the great inquiry of 1796, it had become apparent that the Corporation of the City of London was the most powerful among the opponents of schemes for docks serving ships in the foreign trade. The reason for the Corporation's attitude was that wet docks would have to be excavated downstream of the City boundary, and this would have resulted in the transfer of the most valuable commerce to places outside the jurisdiction of the Corporation.

Nevertheless, the merchants' plan for docks at Wapping, outlined by Vaughan, was responsible for the setting up of the Parliamentary Committee of 1796. The City Corporation, realizing that some scheme of wet docks was inevitable, put forward a plan of its own for a dock on the Isle of Dogs of 102 acres, sufficient to hold 400 ships, and for another of similar size at Rotherhithe. These docks were planned primarily for use by timber ships and colliers, whilst the greater part of foreign cargoes was to be retained at the Legal Quays. Under the Corporation's proposal, these quays were to be extended from their existing 1,500 feet to a frontage of 4,500 feet by means of indentations and five projections into the river.

There were five other plans before the 1796 Committee, but none really tackled the problem of providing for new docks and warehouses for foreign trade. The Committee contented itself with parading the evidence for and against the seven schemes, a task which it performed with admirable objectivity.

The discussions dragged on through four sessions of Parliament, and some West India merchants began to feel that they ought to support a scheme for docks which would have the greatest chance of quick approval rather than retain an inflexible attitude. Undoubtedly, every delay increased their losses through the plunder and bad management which were rife in the port. A compromise was agreed upon with the City Corporation, and the two major interests were able to procure an Act of Parliament for making two docks and a canal across the Isle of Dogs, the latter property to be vested in the Corporation. The West India merchants were not so concerned as the London merchants about the distance of cartage from the proposed docks to the City. The short land haul was one of the chief attractions of the Wapping site proposed by the London merchants.

The first report of the 1799 Parliamentary Committee shows how the climate of opinion had at last been transformed. '... Your Committee would consider any plan for the improvement of the Port imperfect, of which Wet Docks did not make a part. . . .' The Committee in fact recommended both the London merchants' plan for docks at Wapping and the joint scheme for docks across the Isle of Dogs, for the projects were not incompatible. The former would afford the greatest convenience to small ships, and the latter would give the best answer for larger ships in the West India and East India trades.

Preference was given to the Isle of Dogs scheme most probably, as Sir Joseph Broodbank suggests, because of the City's interest in it. It was hoped that the City Canal would provide a much better shipping approach to London itself. The official reasons given by the Committee was that the Isle of Dogs site would obviate the danger and delay of the circuitous passage around the meander enclosing the Isle of Dogs; and there was the smaller space of time within which the docks could be begun and executed compared with the Wapping scheme. The Committee resolved that '. . . the Bill for providing more commodious, and for better regulating, the Port of London, should be proceeded on without further delay. 1 June 1799'.

Dispatch at last entered the proceedings. The *West India Dock Act* received the Royal Assent six weeks later, on July 12, 1799. The first practical move to reduce the intolerable crowding upon the eighteenth century river had begun. Though riverside landing places were to develop remarkably during the following century, henceforth the largest ships were to load and unload not in the river but in docks cut out of its walled-off flood-plain. The river itself was then able to resume more effectively its principal function—that of a water highway to the landing places of the port.

## REFERENCES

1. Sir Joseph Broodbank, *History of the Port of London*, 2 vols. (O'Connor, 1921).

D

2. J. Stow, *A Survey of London, 1603*, 2 vols., edited by C. L. Kingsford (Oxford: Clarendon, 1908). The editor's notes to Vol. II, 6, give a documentation for the following section. A sketch-map of London under Henry II by M. B. Honeybourne is contained in F. M. Stenton, *Norman London*, Historical Association Leaflets (Bell, 1934), 93–4, an important source for Norman London.

3. C. Capper, *The Port and Trade of London* (Smith, Elder, 1862), 50, third footnote.

4. An account of the medieval foreign trade from eastern ports of England, including London, may be found in R. A. Pelham, 'Medieval Foreign Trade: Eastern Ports', *An Historical Geography of England before 1800*, edited by H. C. Darby (Cambridge University Press, 1951), Chapter VII, 298–329. See also E. Power and M. M. Postan, *Studies in English Trade in the Fifteenth Century* (Routledge, 1933).

5. R. A. Pelham, *vide supra*, 325.

6. J. Stow, *op. cit.*, 236, original pagination.

7. Both these yards closed down eventually in 1869 because of the increasing size of H.M. ships. The focus of the Royal Navy's interest on Thameside has now shifted to Wren's Greenwich Hospital which since 1873 has been used as a Royal Naval College.

8. J. Stow, *op. cit.*, 11–12, original pagination.

9. In 1831 the present bridge was completed on a site one hundred feet to the west of the former Old London Bridge which necessitated a new approach from the north via Moorgate and King William Street. This accounts for the present bend in the north-eastern route to the bridge near the Monument Underground Station.

10. J. Stow, *op. cit.*, 12, original pagination.

11. More irregularities to the City boundary have since been added, including a large area west of the Fleet, as far as Temple Bar.

12. The general growth of London during this intervening period is specifically dealt with by O. H. K. Spate, 'The Growth of London, A.D. 1660–1800', *An Historical Geography of England before 1800*, edited by H. C. Darby (Cambridge University Press, 1951), Chapter XIV, 529–47, with a useful bibliographical note.

13. *Report from the Committee appointed to enquire into the Best Mode of providing Sufficient Accommodation for the Increased Trade and Shipping of the Port of London*, May 13, 1796.

14. *Ibid.*, adapted from Appendix D.

15. *Ibid.*, adapted from Appendix H.

16. *Ibid.*, adapted from Appendix G.

17. At a tier a vessel is moored fore and aft to prevent swinging with the tide.

18. *Report* (1796), *op. cit.*, Appendix E and evidence of W. Vaughan. The following is the present definition of 'craft', which gives an idea of its meaning in 1796. 'The expression "craft" means and includes any lighter or barge or other like craft for conveying goods or any tug propelled by steam or any other motive power either wholly or partly within the Port of London . . .', *Port of London* (*Consolidation*) *Act*, 1920, Section 197. The terms lighter and barge are now synonymous.

19. Aspects of this important contributory cause of shipping congestion are studied both on the Thames and at the coal-exporting ports of the north-east coast in L. R. Jones, *The Geography of London River* (Methuen, 1931), 42–7.

20. P. Colquhoun, *A Treatise on the Commerce and Police of the River Thames* (1800), 27.

21. *Report* (1796), *op. cit.*, evidence of Messrs. Ludlam and Walker.

22. Indeed, 300 feet of this must be subtracted as being taken up by water stairs and the coasting trade.

23. See also T. Fallon, *River Police* (Muller, 1956).

24. P. Colquhoun, *op. cit.*, 198.

25. *Ibid.*, facing 22.

26. A. G. Course, *The Place of Tilbury in the Port of London* (P.L.A. MS., 1946), 9.

27. *Report* (1796), *op. cit.*, Appendix I.

# CHAPTER III

# THE WATER HIGHWAY

ALL the port development of London has been made possible by the capacious water highway to the sea. Indeed, Professor Ll. Rodwell Jones (1931), in his study of the tidal Thames, took as his title *The Geography of London River* and discussed the port in the light of the history of the great route.

Amazing as it may appear, although three dock systems had been added to the Port of London, in the first half of the nineteenth century there was no dredging of the river's shoals and banks.

> 'The Corporation of London (although the conservators of the river Thames) contend that they are not by law required to remove such obstructions below bridge, having as they allege, no funds legally applicable to the purpose.'[1]

Not until 1857 were plans made for an integrated programme of channel improvement, but dredging continued in a very desultory fashion. Nevertheless, the interruption of the navigation of the larger vessels did not become really serious until the end of the last century, and then only in certain reaches. It is true to say that up to that time the natural work of the tide kept the port open for all those who wished to use it, and until 1905 there was hardly any *creative* dredging (as opposed to dredging for the removal of specific shoals or to maintain an existing channel).

However, the water route had been artificially improved in another way. A vast work had been carried out, and its first authors have remained anonymous to the historians of the river. The making of the embankments of London River antedates the written record. For the moment, it is sufficient to say that since about the twelfth century the maximum width of the river from London to the sea has been artificially restricted by river walls. Because of this restriction, there has arisen some confusion over the nature of the Thames below London.

NOMENCLATURE

Unfortunately, the meaning of the word 'estuary' is vague. The *Oxford Dictionary* gives the meaning, adapted from the Latin adjective *æstuarium*, as 'the tidal mouth of a great river, where the tide meets the current of fresh water'. Other dictionaries refer to 'the expanding tidal portion of a river'. Because of the vagueness of these meanings, widely differing boundaries are suggested for the landward limit of the Thames Estuary. Hydrographers write of the 'Inner Estuary' ceasing at the eastern end of Sea Reach. P.L.A. experts on the tidal behaviour of the Thames put forward the area between the Gravesend and Lower Hope Reaches as most significant of the change from river to sea. On the other hand, the tide extends right up to Teddington Weir, which might indicate a boundary much further to the west; W. Addison (1954) begins his discussion of the Thames Estuary at London Bridge.

These divergences result from the fact that from the time of its embanking the Thames has had the form of a river in plan, though an examination of its water content might suggest the title of 'canalized marine gulf' over at least part of its length. Before the river walls were built, the energy of the tide spread the water over a much wider area; without doubt, at the highest springs all the present Lower Thameside marshes were under water. The only limits to the width of the gulf would be set by the amount of the floodwater, and the bluffs of the Chalk and the rises of the former flood-plain, especially where these were close to the deepest central channel. Within these limits the great tidal pulse ebbed and flowed at will, untamed by the dwellers of Roman London. Few would deny that at this time the head of the estuary was close to the site of Londinium, where, as has been shown, ground above the flood-plain approaches to within half a mile of each side of the river channel.

Because of a geologically recent rise of sea-level, the tide probably rode roughshod over the earlier meanders which the river had developed. Such meanders as the main channel persisted in were confirmed and fossilized by the construction of river walls. An unruly marine gulf was thereby converted into an embanked tidal river. Therefore, it seems best to designate the present landward limit of the estuary at a point not only where there is a significant widening of the river, but also where the embanked meander pattern comes to an end. The line chosen here is through the Mucking Light between Lower Hope Reach and, appropriately enough, Sea Reach. This limit is readily recognized on the map because to the east of it the Thames no longer has the form of a meandering river in plan. It will be seen later that an examination of water content endorses this siting of what must be a rather arbitrary boundary if a single line is proposed.

The nomenclature adopted here and shown on Figure 1 is as follows: Teddington to London Bridge, *Upper Tidal Thames*; Upper Pool, Lower Pool, and the fifteen reaches downstream, including Lower Hope Reach, *London River*; the banks and marshlands of London River, *Dockland* and *Lower Thameside*; *Sea Reach*; beyond Sea Reach, the *Outer Estuary*; and the shores and marshlands of Sea Reach and the Outer Estuary, the *Estuary Shores and Marshlands*.

Following this attempt to clarify the nomenclature, the discussion which opened this chapter must now be amplified.

EMBANKMENTS

Sir Joseph Broodbank (1921), the historian of the port, was naturally concerned in an attempt to date the first embanking of the river. He judged that it was unlikely that the Romans would construct one hundred miles of embankments when their port was snugly sited away from extensive tracts of flood-plain, their ships of shallow draught, and when their chief line of entry was via Dover, along a road which lay some distance inland from the Thames. Since Domesday Book includes no mention of any settlement on Lower Thameside, it is inferred that the embankments were not constructed by the Anglo-Saxons. There are, however, references to marshlands at Stratford in 1135 and at Erith in 1178; and the earliest statutes about embankments are found in the reign of Henry II which refer to laws of his grandfather, Henry I, who reigned from 1133 until 1189. Evidence from these sources implies that the embanking of the river began in the twelfth century. Since it is in 1324 and 1376 that the earliest recorded river breaches are found, and the first instances of repairs to embankments are quoted for the reign of Edward II,

1284 to 1327,[2] it may be concluded that the embanking of the river was largely completed by the fourteenth century. The vagueness of these dates need cause no surprise. The presumption is that the embanking was carried out in a piecemeal fashion, that flood-plain slowly gave way to saltings which were subsequently drained and became marshlands ; no doubt sectional reclamation proceeded transversely along the river as well as in a parallel fashion towards it.

'All [the walls on the river] began by the protection of property on the earthland foot, and extended piecemeal into the marsh and swamps, so by degrees pushing forward the frontage by a junction of the intervals between salient points. This process being frequently interrupted has produced in some places great irregularity in outline, without, however, preventing the diligent observer from perceiving that the process above-mentioned has in all cases been followed. The popular idea that the present tide-walls at the water's edge were all the result of one effort is the result of ignorance, since there are other obsolete walls which preceded them further inland, and the existing walls are not uniform, presenting irregularities in direction, in form, and construction which precludes any belief in the singleness of design.'[3]

Whole series of these 'obsolete' or counter walls, at right angles to the river, may still be traced.[4] In Sea Reach the dates of reclamation are naturally somewhat later than for Lower Thameside. Canvey Island was not rescued until 1622, when walls were built under the guidance of the Dutch engineer, Cornelius Vermuyden.

A new series of embankments became necessary in the nineteenth century. As the last piers of Old London Bridge crumbled in the river during 1832, tidal energy was increased above its site, because the old bridge had acted as a weir, causing water downstream to be as much as thirteen inches below water upstream. With the final removal of the foundations of this bridge the increased tidal range exposed shoals in the reaches from Southwark to Lambeth, as had been predicted in 1821 by J. Walker. The following quotes his evidence from the *Report of the*

*Select Committee on the State of London Bridge*, 1821, Appendix I.

> 'We have stated that the tide of flood [upon the removal of
> Old London Bridge] will rise higher than at present. . . .
> The great cause of shoals is the unequal velocity of
> current, and this inequality increases as the velocity increases;
> . . . The means we should recommend [to combat shoals above
> the bridge] are, the nearer approximation to a uniform vel-
> ocity, which would best be accomplished by producing an
> equality of area, such as contracting the width of the river
> abreast of the shoals, by means of embankments or other-
> wise; . . .'

Here is the seed of the idea for the London embankments.

Another separate reason for their construction was the need
to supply a site for the low-level sewers planned by the Metropolitan Board of Works in 1858.[5] Their chief engineer, Mr. (later
Sir) Joseph Bazalgette, drew up the plans for the main drainage of
the metropolis, and the Act for the construction of embankments
above London Bridge was passed in 1863. The Albert Embankment was completed in 1869, the Victoria in 1870, and the Chelsea
in 1874. The greater uniformity in the width of the river thus
achieved helped to improve navigation on the Upper Tidal
Thames; moreover, much infilling for the area behind the walls
was dredged from the contiguous reaches of the river.

The present river walls, downstream from the area of continuously built-up river frontage, are the descendants of the
early dikes of Plantagenet times. Today they generally consist
on the river side of a revetment of Kentish Ragstone and Block
Chalk, about twenty inches thick, which covers a clay hearting.
The crest is about four feet wide and usually provides a path for
pedestrians. The walls need the constant attention of the River
Boards. Like natural features they are subject to weathering; the
underlying peat and alluvium are compressible; and there is a
natural tendency for the walls to slip towards the river on the
side where there is little opportunity to buttress the foundations.
These embankments are not continuous, because, as was shown
in Chapter I, higher land abuts on the river at several places on

the south bank, and where there are riverside industrial or wharf premises special and private embanking is the rule.

Throughout the recorded history of the river these embankments have fulfilled two great functions. The main channels of the Thames were deepened and maintained by the confined and resultant increased vigour of the tidal scour; and land below the level of high tides has been made safe and available for development. The Lower Thameside Marshes are in fact the remnants of the deposits of the marine gulf which was the forerunner of London River. The depth of these estuarine silts, in which beds of peat and marsh clay occur, increases eastwards from fifteen feet at Charing Cross to forty feet at Tilbury Docks. No doubt shrinkage has occurred since the original draining, but it is to be expected that these lands should be well below high tide level. In fact, they are generally only three to four feet above O.D. and before the nineteenth century were used chiefly for pasture. Then came the excavation of wet docks, and in the last seventy years about a quarter of the area of marshland has provided sites for industrial development of one kind or another (Chapter VII). However, until relatively recently, the borders of London River were isolated because of the unstable terrain for building, lack of building materials or shelter, and their damp nature which rendered them unhealthy. Malaria was not finally expunged from the estuary marshes until late in the nineteenth century.

THE TIDE

As a consequence of this embanking, tidal energies have become concentrated upon a smaller cross-section of water. The tide which affects the Thames starts as an oscillation in the southern half of the North Sea. Under the influence of the earth's rotation, the oscillation revolves around a central amphidromic (or non-tidal) point. The co-tidal lines of Figure 4 show that the tidal range increases outwards from this point, and that in the Outer Estuary of the Thames the range is normally twelve feet. The isochronous high water lines betray the anti-clockwise revolution of the oscillation and show how the flood tide flows into the estuary, parallel to the Essex shore, and then up London River. Times of local high water occur therefore progressively

later in a westward direction. Figure 5 shows that the range of
the tide actually increases from Southend to London Bridge,
because although the kinetic tidal energy is being dissipated by
friction and the counter movement of land water, it is being

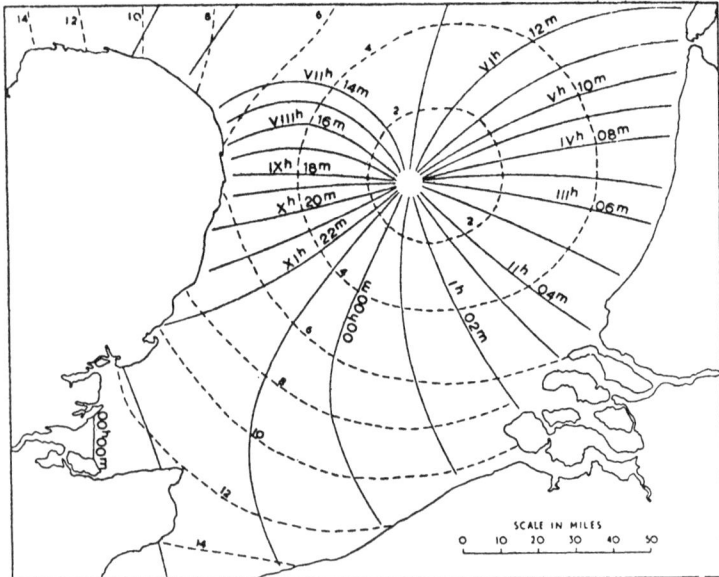

FIG. 4.—Propagation of Tides in the Southern Half of the North Sea.
The continuous lines represent places with high water at the same time;
the broken lines represent places with the same tidal range.
Based upon Admiralty Chart No. 5058 with the permission of the Controller of H.M.
Stationery Office and of the Hydrographer of the Navy.

expended on a decreasing embanked cross-section. Beyond
London Bridge the latter effect is no longer sufficient to overcome
the former, and the tidal range falls off rapidly. The oscillation
is of a semi-diurnal type, and at any one place the times of a.m.
and p.m. local high water are retarted by about fifty minutes
daily.

The tide is the pulse of the port. Not only does it increase
periodically the depth of water in the channels, but it helps to

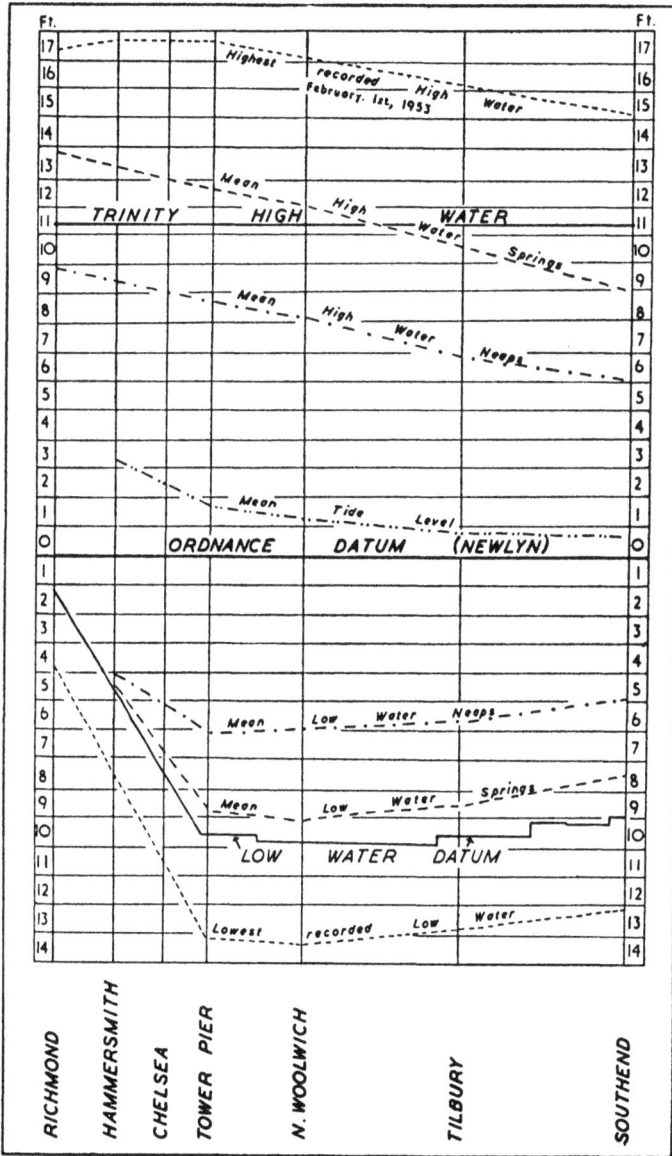

Fig. 5.—Tidal Ranges in the Thames.

keep them clear by its natural scour; and the movement of the tidal currents is an auxiliary motor for the smaller craft. The speed of these currents depends on the type of tide, the width of the reach, and the time relative to high or low water. On one tide craft could reckon to move nine to fifteen miles on tidal currents with speeds from just under two knots (at neaps in wide reaches on the ebb tide) to a maximum of five knots (at springs in narrow reaches on the flood). Large liners bound for the Royal Docks generally depart from Gravesend at or about low water and up to two hours after low water, depending on the draught of the vessel. The ship is then able to come up on the early flood, taking about one and a half hours to the Royal Docks. Ships arrive off the lock well before high water, the tidal crest, though travelling faster, failing to catch them *en route* from Gravesend.

WATER CONTENT

Discussion of the mechanism of the tide leads naturally to an enquiry into the water content of London River. Is there any way of determining to what extent this is a true river, a carrier of land water to the sea, and to what extent is it merely a gutter for the reception of sea water overflowed by the tide? In practice the problem is complicated by the fact that the Metropolitan Water Board abstracts 7,000 million gallons per month (average for 1954) from the river at Teddington, which may be as much as a third of the summer flow. On the other hand, below Teddington, apart from the natural tributaries, much land drainage and sewage effluent are discharged from the Northern (Barking) and Southern (Cross Ness) Outfalls; the monthly average for these outfalls for 1954 was practically 9,000 million gallons. Two-thirds of this enormous quantity was discharged at the Northern Outfall, the biggest tributary of the Thames, not excluding the Medway.[6]

A method of discovering water content which allows for the varying factors is to take a series of salinity samples. If the salinity values obtained for various points in the Thames are compared with the average value for the North Sea, it is possible to calculate the proportion of sea water to land water for that particular point at that particular time relative to high water.

Measurements by the L.C.C. over long periods have shown that in the Thames the vertical mixing of sea and land water is intense and that there is only a slight stratification between them. In other words a salinity measurement at one particular depth may be taken as the measurement for the whole vertical cross-section. Since there is little salinity variation in a cross-section, it may be assumed that water of a constant salinity moves with the tide, and therefore all measurements within a short period of time can be converted to the same time, relative to local high water. W. S. Preddy (1954) has produced such a corrected salinity curve for the Thames based on the average contents of chloride for the period from January 1 to December 18, 1948. Here it will be convenient if the annual average percentages of sea water in the various reaches are deduced from this smooth curve:

TABLE VI

*Average Percentages of Sea Water in London River during 1948*

| | % | | | % |
|---|---|---|---|---|
| At London Bridge | ... 3 | Erith Reach ... | ... | 38 |
| Limehouse Reach | ... 6 | Erith Rands ... | ... | 41 |
| Greenwich Reach | ... 11 | Long Reach ... | ... | 46 |
| Blackwall Reach | ... 14 | St. Clements Reach | ... | 52 |
| Bugsby's Reach ... | ... 19 | Northfleet Hope | ... | 56 |
| Woolwich Reach | ... 22 | Gravesend Reach | ... | 62 |
| Gallions Reach ... | ... 26 | Lower Hope Reach | ... | 69 |
| Barking Reach ... | ... 30 | At Mucking Light | ... | 73 |
| Halfway Reach ... | ... 35 | | | |

Of course these proportions are subject to great fluctuations, of short duration with the tide, and of a longer term with the variations in fresh water flow over Teddington Weir. With a high winter flow of land water, the figures may be reduced by a greater amount progressively eastward. For instance, during the week ended January 22, 1955, the proportion of sea water at the Mucking Light was only 45%. It is not inappropriate that this limit, which was taken to be the eastern boundary of London River, should cross the zone where land and sea water are approximately equal when the river is in flood.

FLOODS

The height of the tide cannot always be predicted exactly because of the irregularity of the flow of land water over Teddington Weir and the aperiodic storm surges in the North Sea. Over the tidal portion of the Thames itself, tides tend to be diminished by westerly winds and increased by easterlies.

The unified control of the waterway achieved under the P.L.A. is not matched on Thameside. Responsibility for flood prevention and land drainage continued to be divided among a number of local authorities and Commissioners of Sewers until the Land Drainage Act of 1930 set up a series of Drainage and Catchment Boards. Further simplification took place with the passing of the *River Boards Act* in 1948. Even so, in the County of London and downstream there are no less than six riparian authorities concerned with the regime of this waterway.

Forty square miles of the Lower Thames Marshes are the natural flood-plain of London River and the Thames Estuary; the word flood-plain must be interpreted literally, for while embanking restricts the lateral development of a tide, it increases the height of tides, including of course the highest tide. These will inevitably spill over into parts of the flood-plain.

The *Report of the Departmental Committee on Coastal Flooding.* (Cmd. 9165, 1954) stated:

> 'The cost of affording protection against the worst possibilities would be colossal and we have ruled out any idea of being able to recommend measures designed to secure complete protection against every conceivable tide and surge.'[7]

In the County of London, after the 1928 floods, defences were fixed at seventeen to eighteen feet above O.D. The January 1953 floods capped the top of these defences, even though the flow over Teddington Weir was low for that time of the year and the peak of the storm surge did not coincide with local high water. Serious breaches occurred downstream because the defences were fixed at heights decreasing to fifteen and a half feet above O.D. in Sea Reach. Below the County of London 40,000 acres of land were flooded, with the flooding at its worst downstream, including the inundation of Canvey Island with the loss of fifty-seven lives.

The maximum standard of protection recommended by the Waverley Committee in 1954 was in general to be

> 'that sufficient to withstand the flood of January, 1953, and this should be provided where flooding would affect a large area of valuable agricultural land, or would lead to serious damage of property of high value such as valuable industrial premises or compact residential areas. Elsewhere, the defences should be at a standard thought adequate before the flood of January, 1953.'[8]

Where the riverside has been fully built up it is impossible to make addition to the defences without enormous cost; this applies with the greatest force in the Pools and for the embankments and built-up frontages above London Bridge.

In the last hundred years the levels of the highest previous tide have been exceeded with increasing frequency. The following are the records of the tidal gauge at Southend, all converted to heights above O.D.[9]

|           |      |     |     |     |            |
|-----------|------|-----|-----|-----|------------|
| November, | 1897 | ... | ... | ... | 13·6 feet  |
| January,  | 1928 | ... | ... | ... | 13·6 ,,    |
| February, | 1938 | ... | ... | ... | 13·7 ,,    |
| March,    | 1949 | ... | ... | ... | 13·8 ,,    |
| January,  | 1953 | ... | ... | ... | 15·4 ,,    |

An analysis of these high levels shows that they are not due to increases in the height of the tides themselves, but to increases in the height of the associated surges. Part of the resultant rise is due possibly to further embanking during the last hundred years; another factor is probably the steady rise of mean sea-level relative to the land, estimated to be about eight inches per century in south-east England. Moreover, with a higher flow of land water at Teddington and with a nearer superimposition of a surge upon local high water, a much greater height than the 1953 flood is to be expected.

However, the picture is not really so sombre. The statistical chance of a recurrence of the flood level of January 1953 is reckoned to be once in two hundred years. It is obviously uneconomic to improve the defences much further. The risk to human life can be almost eliminated by a flood warning system such as that recommended in the *Interim Report* of the Waverley Committee (1954). Yet there remains the threat to riverside property including industrial and port installations. This brief discussion should serve to illustrate the fact that though the Thames may be an excellent servant for 199 years, in that two-hundredth year it will be a terrible master. No one can predict this 'two-hundredth' year. It is the inevitable penalty that the port must pay for its tenancy of a flood-plain.

## THE NAVIGABLE CHANNELS

There have been three conservators of London River and the Thames Estuary: the Corporation of the City of London, from 1197 to 1857; the Thames Conservancy, from 1857 to 1909; and the P.L.A. A discussion of the government of the river and the navigable channels within it may be conveniently treated with reference to these three administrative regimes.

The chief features of the City's period of conservancy are its length, the fact that during the whole time practically nothing was done to improve the navigable channels, and the protracted legal battle with the Crown which accompanied the end of its authority. In 1797 an elaborate defence of the vesting of the conservancy in the City Corporation was made in the House of Commons. The Town Clerk stated that amongst other bases it depended on a prescription by the Exchequer Court in 1605; on six ancient charters, the first dated 1197; and on five Acts of Parliament, the first dated 1394.

In 1771 the duties of the Lord Mayor and his water bailiffs were taken over by a Port Committee of the Corporation.[10] This Committee, however, contended (*see* above, p. 52) that they were not by law required to remove obstructions below London Bridge. It is true that since the seventeenth century Trinity House had had the exclusive right of ballastage, but this scarcely improved the river channels. The Trinity House dredgers kept within ten miles of the Pools and only raised clean sand and gravel; and the shoals of mud impeding the channels were entirely ignored. In 1707 a notable shoal occurred in Halfway Reach, following on the Dagenham Breach of that year. Its removal was effected by ballast-men, but their contracts from the City Corporation were for this specific job. There is little doubt that the Port Committee of the Corporation was quite inefficient. Many of its members were traders who had little knowledge or experience of navigational problems.

The recommendations of the *Report from the Select Committee on the Port of London*, 1836, stand as an implicit condemnation of the City's rule over the river. Yet nothing was done to set up a specialist conservancy board until 1857. Two main reasons have been suggested for this delay. In the first place river traffic decreased during this period, and congestion on the river was reduced. This was due to the gradual replacement of sailing vessels by those driven by steam, the wet docks (which reduced the crowding of the river berths), and the diversion of much coastwise traffic to the railways. Secondly, all ᵼne energies of the Crown, as far as the Thames was concerned, were concentrated on a battle with the City Corporation as to which of them had the rights to the bed, soil, and shores of the Thames. This legal wrangle was ended in 1857 with the establishment of the Thames Conservancy Board with jurisdiction over the whole river from the source to Yantlet Creek, half-way along Sea Reach. By this time London River had certain navigational defects for vessels using the port.

At the beginning of the nineteenth century East Indiamen might draw as much as twenty-five feet. Yet in 1857 the twenty-four-foot and eighteen-foot L.W.S.T.[11] channels ceased in Erith Rands; in Barking Reach the limiting depth was twelve feet; and from Woolwich to Limehouse it was only nine to ten feet.[12] Accordingly, the Indiamen had to be lightened to seventeen feet in Long Reach. At the eastern end of London River, in Lower Hope Reach, the limiting depth was twenty-three feet. The critical parts of the Lower Hope Reach and Erith Rands occurred where the meanders of London River cross the Purfleet and Cliffe anticlines of Chalk (Chapter I).

The Thames Conservancy began a programme of dredging and, according to the *Report of the Select Committee on Thames*

E

*Conservancy*, 1863, had removed the irregular shoals above Barking Creek. By 1888 the twenty-six-foot channel extended to Tilbury Docks, the eighteen-foot channel to the Royal Albert Dock, and the fourteen-foot channel to the upper docks.

Yet this considerable improvement had not kept pace with the demands of shipowners; about this time the complaints against the inadequacy of the river channels came to be crystallized around a demand for a channel of thirty feet L.W.S.T. As this was considerably in excess of the capacity of the upper reaches of London River and was not even attained below Gravesend, the Board of Trade set up the Lower Thames Navigation Commission in 1894. The Thames Conservators in evidence before it stated that their programme was a twenty-four-foot channel to Erith Rands, twenty-two feet to the Royal Albert Dock Entrance, and thence eighteen feet to London Bridge. The London Association of Shipowners and Brokers had based their demands for thirty feet on the following: the Suez Canal was about to be deepened to thirty feet, Southampton had just completed a channel of thirty feet right into the dock, and the larger vessels using the port frequently had a loaded draught of over thirty feet.

The Commission came to the conclusion that the shipowners were right, that a thirty-foot channel ought to be provided to Gravesend at least, and if possible this should be extended to the Royal Albert Dock. This was a wise conclusion, for in a world port like London the facilities available should anticipate by some years the likely demands of ships. Unfortunately, the Conservators did not take the recommendations of the Commission to be mandatory. They adhered to their original programme, though with the funds from the *Thames Conservancy Act*, 1905, they were directed to provide a channel 1,000 feet by 30 feet to Gravesend. The delay is apparent. At a critical time of shipping development the port was beginning to lag behind the demands of vessels. This was a most serious situation.

Yet by that Act of 1905 a new era for the waterway was opened. In 1857 dredging had been mainly concerned with ameliorating or rectifying the existing channel; henceforth, the task was to construct deeper channels aligned to take the best advantage of tidal scour. Soon after, a dredging programme was commended to the newly established P.L.A. and this was largely completed by 1925, as the following shows:

TABLE VII

*Shipping Channel Programme, 1908, and Present Channels, London Bridge to the Sea*

*All Depths are L.W.S.T.*

| *Programme (Recommendations of Joint Engineers' Report, 1908)* | *Present Channels*[13] |
|---|---|
| London Bridge to Greenland Dock: 400–500 ft. by 14–16 ft. | London Bridge to Tower Bridge: 300–350 ft. by 14 ft. |
| | Tower Bridge to Thames Tunnel, Wapping (see front endpaper): 400 ft. by 14 ft. |
| | Thames Tunnel to Greenland Dock: 400–600 ft. by 16 ft. |
| Greenland Dock to Royal Albert Dock: 600 ft. by 20 ft. | Greenland Dock to King George V Dock: 450–600 ft. by 20 ft. |
| Royal Albert Dock to Coldharbour Point (between Erith Reach and Erith Rands): 600 ft. by 30 ft. | King George V Dock to Coldharbour Point: 600 ft. by 27 ft. |
| Coldharbour Point to Sea Reach Buoy No. 1: 1,000 ft. by 30 ft. | Coldharbour Point to Sea Reach Buoy No. 1: 1,000 ft. by 30 ft. |

The annual dredging bill borne by the P.L.A. in the year ended March 31, 1954, reached £687,641 (4.6% of total P.L.A. expenditure), and the following shows that there are a few areas which are particularly troublesome:

TABLE VIII

*Average Percentages of Total Dredging, April 1, 1950, to March 31, 1955*

(3 million hopper tons per annum approx.)

| | | | | | | | |
|---|---|---|---|---|---|---|---|
| Royal Docks ... | ... | ... | ... | ... | ... | 14 | |
| The 'Mud Reaches' (Gallions, Barking, Halfway) ... | | | | | | 13 | |
| Tilbury Tidal Basin ... | ... | ... | ... | ... | 14 | } 66 |
| Gravesend Reach ... | ... | ... | ... | ... | 25 | |
| Elsewhere ... | ... | ... | ... | ... | ... | 34 | |

Since the enormous cost of dredging in the port is to a large extent concentrated in the four areas specified above, the problem of silting is less indeterminate than might have been supposed.

The need to study the silting of these areas was one of the reasons for building the tidal model of the Thames in number 8 shed, Royal Victoria Dock. The vertical scale of the model is 1 :60 and there is a horizontal scale of 1 :600, which necessitates a miniature waterway about 400 feet long.

In July 1955 radioactive tracers were injected into the river opposite the Tilbury Tidal Basin. Geiger counters detected some of these tracers in the 'Mud Reaches'. They had moved with mud in suspension near the river bed, and thus was demonstrated the importance of landward river bed drift under low river flow conditions.[14]

Apart from increased depths, another less obvious advance achieved by modern dredging is the smoothing of curves around the meanders. The natural channels, used up to the middle of the nineteenth century, had sharper bends than the river shorelines would suggest because of the tendency for a stream to undercut part of the concave banks and to deposit material on the shoulders of the convexities.

Beyond London River, in Sea Reach, the Yantlet Dredged Channel runs within 1,500 feet of the Essex shore past Thameshaven and Canvey Island. Thence it curves almost imperceptibly to the south to run midway between the shores until it crosses the seaward limit of the P.L.A. at Sea Reach Buoy No. 1 (Figure 1).

It is here that the Outer Estuary begins, and a characteristic which distinguishes it from London River and Sea Reach is the fact that all the navigable channels are natural. Here the Essex and Kent shores diverge widely eastwards and between them a threefold division of the submarine morphology may be recognized (Figure 6).[15]

In the south, as marine and sub-aerial erosion attacked the coast of Kent, formed of London Clay, it retreated quite rapidly. The end-product of this erosion is a wave-cut platform called The Cant and Kentish Flats, an area of comparatively shallow water of less than 18 feet L.W.S.T. Secondly, to the north-west, where the Maplin Sands might be considered a counterpart of the Cant and Kentish Flats, the most notable feature is a series of channels and associated banks from Gunfleet in the north-west to Long Sand in the south-east. The third division is noted

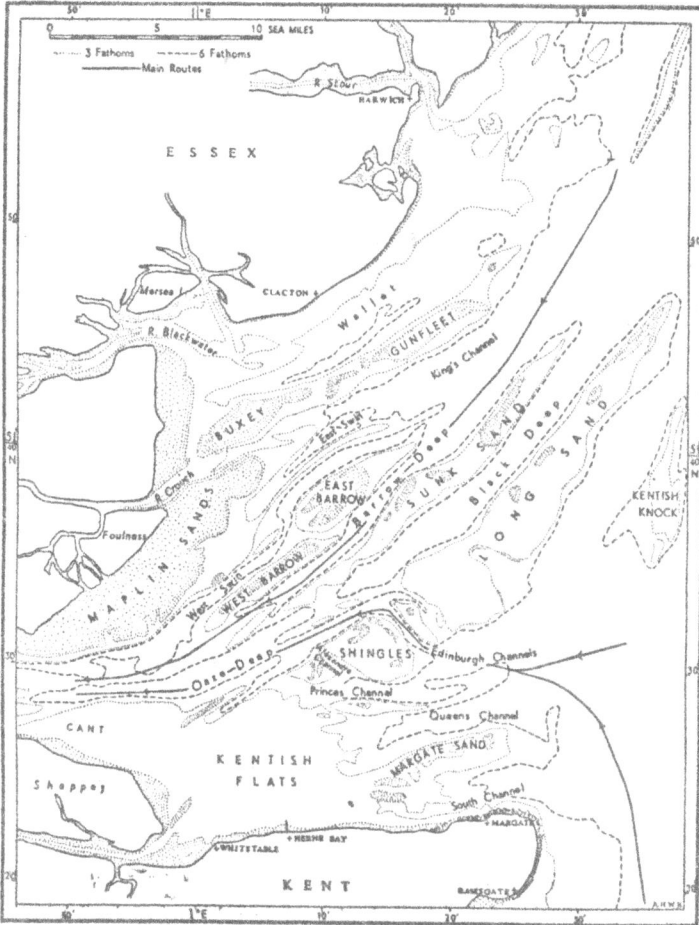

FIG. 6.—The Outer Estuary.

After a diagram by A. H. W. Robinson (1951), reproduced by permission of the Institute of Navigation, and based upon Admiralty Charts Nos. 1607 and 1975 with the permission of the Controller of H.M. Stationery Office and of the Hydrographer of the Navy.

where the southern half of Long Sand is crossed by a number of transverse swatchways (Saxon, *swaeth*, a track).

This pattern has come about as the result of the work of marine erosion upon river and glacial deposits. These consist of unconsolidated material now operated upon by tidal streams. The movement of the North Sea tide is responsible for the alignment of the banks along the Essex coast, and the swatchways across Long Sand seem to be the work of the English Channel tide which enters the Outer Estuary when the energy of the south-westward flowing stream has passed its peak. This helps to explain why Long Sand, which is nearest to the sphere of propagation of the English Channel tide, has been cut by the largest and most permanent swatchways.

Over this rather complicated submarine relief, different navigation routes have been followed as the tonnage of vessels increased and as hydrographic knowledge of the estuary became more complete. The migration has taken place from the days when shipping kept within sight of landmarks as far as possible. The route from the north has merely moved to a deeper and more seaward channel of those which run parallel to the Essex coast; this was because silting in the inner channels became an embarrassment, especially the growth of the Middle Swin Bar. Black Deep is reserved as a dumping ground for the sludge constituent of London's sewage and for the material dredged from the river.

The West Swin and Oaze Deep are ebb channels, which have the characteristic of shoaling away from the land; all the others are flood channels which shoal towards the land. Difficulties for navigation occur when vessels proceed across the shallow water sill between the two types of channel: *i.e.* the Middle Swin Bar in the north (*see* above), and the bars extending from the Shingles Patch shoal for the southern route (*see* below).[16]

This southern route has had a more complicated history than the route from the north. The larger ships of the East India Company (800 tons, 18 feet draught laden; 1,200 tons, 25 feet draught laden) first became embarrassed by the shoals of the Kentish Flats in the eighteenth century. G. Spence wrote in the *Nautical Description of Banks and Channels* (1804) that 'Men of War and Indiamen were forced to sail through the King's Channel and round Long Sand Head' on the way from London to the Downs. This was a detour of fifty miles.

However, in 1775, the first use had been made of the transverse swatchways in Long Sand—the Queen's Channel. In the middle of the nineteenth century Prince's Channel was used. In 1889 a channel was buoyed and named after the then Master of Trinity House, the Duke of Edinburgh. In the centre of this swatchway there developed a shoal called the Shingles Patch, so that by 1921 there were two channels: the North Edinburgh and the South Edinburgh. During the decade following, the North Edinburgh Channel began to shoal, and since then the South Edinburgh Channel has provided the principal track for ships using the southern route. Prince's Channel is normally used by shallower draughted coastal vessels. Recent survey indicates that the North Edinburgh Channel is deepening once more.

The seaward limit of the P.L.A. is very real for shipping. Until incoming ships reach it they take a course over the natural sea bed, guided by the buoys and beacons of Trinity House to take the shortest and deepest channel which the submarine relief allows. West of that limit over 500 ships a week travel along a water highway constructed and maintained by the authority of the port whither they are bound.

## REFERENCES

1. *Report from the Select Committee on the Port of London*, 1836, evidence of Sir John Hall, 23. This evidence was confirmed by the chairman of the Port and Navigation Committee of the Corporation, *ibid.*, 70.

2. Sir William Dugdale, *History of Imbanking and Draining* (2nd edition, 1772), 59 and 74.

3. F. C. J. Spurrell, 'Account of an Excursion to Higham', *Proceedings of the Geologists' Association*, 2 (1889–90), lxxiii–iv.

4. B. E. Cracknell, *The Alluvial Marshlands of the Lower Thames Estuary* (Unpublished thesis, Ph.D., University of London, 1953), Figure 4.

5. A. F. Green, 'The Problem of London's Drainage', *Geography*, XLI (1956), 149–54, and Figure 1.

6. *Ibid.*, 153

7. The extracts are quoted by permission of the Controller of H.M. Stationery Office.

8. *Report of the Departmental Committee on Coastal Flooding* (Cmd. 9165, H.M.S.O., 1954), 29. In Essex and Kent the total sum spent on flood prevention since 1953 is £15 million. B. E. Cracknell, *P.L.A. Monthly*, XXI (1956), 356–9, reports that the river walls have been raised by about three feet between Purfleet and Tilbury, and around the Sea Reach oil refineries, Canvey Island, and the western part of the Isle of Sheppey.

9. *Ibid.*, 6.

10. Although to this day the Lord Mayor of London still claims the title of Admiral of the Port of London.

11. These figures, and those which follow, were the depths at low water of spring tides. When the tide is taken into account, depths of more than seven feet at neaps and nine feet at springs, operating for five to six hours, can be added to these L.W.S.T. figures.

12. L. R. Jones, *The Geography of London River* (Methuen, 1931), 34 *et seq.*, and 119.

13. The lighting, buoyage, and pilotage in these channels continue to be carried out by the 400-year-old Trinity House Authority.

14. F. H. Allen and J. Grindley, 'Radioactive Tracers in the Thames Estuary', *The Dock and Harbour Authority*, 37 (1957), 302–6.

15. A. H. W. Robinson, 'The Changing Navigation Routes of the Thames Estuary', *Journal of the Institute of Navigation*, IV (1951), 357–70; and *The Thames Estuary: a Regional Hydrographic Study* (Unpublished thesis, M.Sc., University of London, 1952).

16. For a discussion of the submarine morphology of the estuary in the light of the ebb-flood channel theory of J. Van Veen, see A. H. W. Robinson, 'The Submarine Morphology of Certain Port Approach Systems', *Journal of the Institute of Navigation*, IX (1956), 20–46.

# CHAPTER IV

# THE OLDER DOCKS

1. *India and Millwall Docks*
2. *London and St. Katharine Docks*

THE passing of the *West India Dock Act* in 1799 inaugurated the era of private dock companies in the Port of London which lasted for over a century until the setting up of the P.L.A. in 1909. The promotions of eight original dock companies had by this time resulted in the existence of five distinct dock systems, and the pedigree of the P.L.A. on the next page shows the progressive integrations of the dock interests in the port.[1]

The reasons for the major amalgamations may be briefly summarized.

1838 The East and West India Dock Companies combined in order to meet competition from the London and St. Katharine Dock Companies. When the East India Docks were built they were not equipped with warehouses, because the East India Company which owned them had its own warehouses in and near the City. The West India Dock warehouses proved to have surplus accommodation. These complementary characteristics were a further inducement to amalgamation.

1864 The London and St. Katharine Docks, with no railway connection, relatively small entrance locks, and shallow river channels of access, had extensive warehouse accommodation. The Victoria Dock, opened in 1855, had opposite characteristics. Combination between the three docks was mutually advantageous and met competition from the first amalgamation.

1889 The East and West India Dock Company's income was below working expenses, chiefly due to the early failure of the Tilbury Docks opened in 1886. A first combination with the London and St. Katharine Docks Company

73

TABLE IX

*The Pedigree of the P.L.A.*

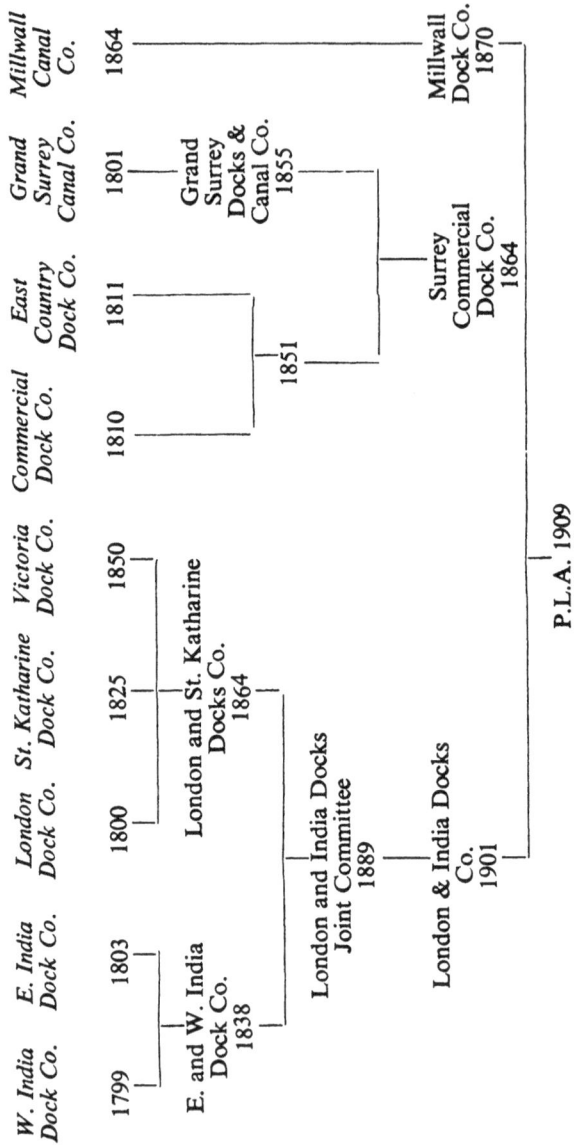

| W. India Dock Co. | E. India Dock Co. | London Dock Co. | St. Katharine Dock Co. | Victoria Dock Co. | Commercial Dock Co. | East Country Dock Co. | Grand Surrey Canal Co. | Millwall Canal Co. |
|---|---|---|---|---|---|---|---|---|
| 1799 | 1803 | 1800 | 1825 | 1850 | 1810 | 1811 | 1801 | 1864 |

E. and W. India Dock Co. 1838

London and St. Katharine Docks Co. 1864

1851

Grand Surrey Docks & Canal Co. 1855

London and India Docks Joint Committee 1889

Surrey Commercial Dock Co. 1864

Millwall Dock Co. 1870

London & India Docks Co. 1901

P.L.A. 1909

provided for joint administration, but the capital of each company remained separate. The East and West India Dock Company received 31% of the profits up to £475,000. Above this figure profits were shared.

1901 Full amalgamation of the above companies met the demands of the East and West India Docks Board which had proved the more adventurous element in the Joint Committee. This was because, with less capital involved, it only risked 31% of any loss but stood to gain half any excess profits.

1909 A major cause of the setting up of the P.L.A. was the need for a comprehensive control of the river in order to provide a sufficient river channel to the dock systems (*see* Chapter III). Further aspects of the P.L.A. are discussed in Chapter IX.

In this and the following chapter each of the dock systems, now administered by the P.L.A., is described as follows : after a brief genetic description of the water area of the system, an imaginary tour is made around the docks to describe their functions. This 'tour' will proceed, as far as possible, in a clockwise direction from the north-west corner of the dock or system. Since most of the dock operations can be related to a quayside installation, constant reference will be made to the buildings shown on the front and back endpapers. Descent into detail,

TABLE X

*Dimensions of the Port of London's Dock Systems*

| Dock System | Total Area (acres) | Water Area (acres) | Dimensions (in feet) of Principal Entrance Lock | | | Total Length of Quay (miles) |
| | | | Length | Width | Depth² | |
|---|---|---|---|---|---|---|
| India and Millwall | 515 | 155 | 584 | 80 | 35 | 8 |
| London and St. Katharine ... | 125½ | 45 | 350 | 60 | 28 | 4 |
| Surrey Commercial | 381½ | 134 | 550 | 80 | 35¼ | 8¼ |
| Royal Docks ... | 1,112 | 235 | 800 | 100 | 45 | 10 |
| Tilbury ... ... | 725 | 104 | 1,000 | 110 | 45½ | 4 |

where the account deals with a single structure, should not be wondered at; important functions in the port may be controlled or carried out in a surprisingly small number of buildings which though large in reality appear quite small on maps covering large areas of the port.

General points about dock operation will be discussed where they first arise in the course of the itinerary.[3] Emphasis will be placed on the docks themselves rather than on the goods which pass through them. These will be treated in more detail later (Chapter VIII). Each section will conclude with a brief note on an area adjacent to that particular dock system.


1. INDIA AND MILLWALL DOCKS (*see* front endpaper)

The system under the above title now consists of the West India Docks (opened 1802), the Millwall Docks (1868), and the one remaining East India Dock (1806). Though sited on the formerly deserted Isle of Dogs marshes, part of the Thames flood-plain, the docks are situated only three to four miles downstream from the City of London boundary. The foundations of these docks in the alluvium was greatly assisted by the occurrence of a gravel layer called Thames Ballast, about 20 feet thick, 16 feet below O.D. This is in fact an old buried channel of the Thames.[4]

The Import and Export Docks are the docks originally specified by the *West India Dock Act* of 1799. The separation of imported cargoes from those due for export was in order to meet objections by the Commissioners of Customs to levying duty on both classes of goods in one dock area. The South West India Dock was created in 1829 from the City Canal and widened in the period 1866–70. The original canal across the Isle of Dogs was part of the price paid for the City Corporation's co-sponsorship of the West India Dock plans. The canal proved a failure; though it shortened the distance to the Upper and Lower Pools, there was no saving in time.

The West India and Millwall Docks have been intercommunicating since 1929, and the principal entrance has been via the Upper Blackwall lock to the South West India Dock. The Lower Blackwall Entrance, of more modest dimensions (*see* front endpaper), is a valuable asset since it enables coastal vessels and barges to be docked, thus relieving pressure on the principal lock.

The Blackwall Basin is typical of many such basins behind the older locks. They date from the time when they were used for crowding in small sailing vessels. The gates to the river were opened a little before high tide and the vessels hauled in and out until high tide when the river gates were closed, and perhaps twenty vessels proceeded to their berths in the dock. This saved the delay that would have been occasioned by locking in and out many small vessels one at a time.

The Poplar Docks, part of which originally functioned as two reservoirs to keep up a head of water in the West India Docks, were leased by the East and West India Dock Company to the North London Railway Company on a 999 years' lease from 1850. This agreement was negotiated to give the dock company a link with the Midlands and the north. The legatees of this contract, the P.L.A. and British Railways (London Midland and Eastern Regions), continue the arrangement. Other regions of British Railways likewise find that an outlet on the Thames is essential to complete their transport net.[5] By this means they are able to cheapen the cost of moving goods to and from vessels in docks by taking advantage of the 'free water' privileges enjoyed by barge traffic (*see* Chapter VI).

The chief function of the Junction Dock, south of the Blackwall Basin, is the provision of barge berths for craft lightering timber from other docks and from other parts of this system.

From the South West India Dock a cut now leads shipping to the reversed 'L' of the Millwall Docks. The Millwall Entrance in Limehouse Reach, shown on the map, was damaged during the war and has not been reopened. This is not surprising for its use would entail a detour of two and a half miles upstream of the Upper Blackwall Entrance.

The East India Docks were constructed for use of vessels of the East India Company, on the site of the ancient Brunswick Dock, and, like the West India Docks, consisted of a basin (*see* back endpaper) communicating with an Import and an Export Dock. The modest dimensions of the entrance lock make it the smallest dock entrance in the port. The Export Dock area was sold by the P.L.A., and since 1951 the site has been occupied by the Brunswick Electricity Generating Station.

A descriptive tour now begins at the north-west corner of the West India Docks. Of the original massive range of eleven warehouses which lined the northern quay of the West India Import Dock, only 1 and parts of 2 and 11 warehouses remain after the destruction of the Second World War. All the original warehouses were protected by a formidable wall, lengths of which are still visible, to guard against the plunder which West Indian goods had previously suffered on the river. A. G. Linney (1930), in describing the West India Docks, headed a chapter, appropriately enough, 'The Dock that was a Fortress'. In 1 and 2, which are partially bonded warehouses, unrefined sugar is stored, and they are so far back from the water because in 1912 a false quay was built out into the dock to increase the quay width by fifty-six feet. Another advantage of such a false quay is that it has a vertical face, in place of the concave curve of the original wall, and gives a greater available depth immediately alongside the quay.

C, D, and E are transit sheds, principally dealing with imports from the four north quay berths of the Import Dock. Transit sheds differ from warehouses in that the goods normally remain in them only for a matter of a few days, compared with weeks, months, or even years in warehouses. Transit sheds are necessary because land and water transport cannot be completely synchronized. Many goods could not just be dumped on the quay and left. They must be taken under cover, sorted, and often made up into special lots according to the requirements of their next destination. In warehouses a longer sojourn may give time for much more complicated operations to be performed. Warehouses do not need to be close to the water's edge. Indeed, they may derive some advantage from being inland of the importing transit shed where some preliminary sorting can be carried out. However, the India and Millwall Docks are not now the most important warehousing docks of the port, and a consideration of the principles involved in port warehousing may be conveniently deferred until the discussion of the next dock system.

On the south side of the Import Dock the buildings marked 6 to 11 serve East Wood Wharf, the traditional centre of the hardwood trade in the Port of London. There are now only eight (five original and three reconstructed) sheds out of a pre-war total of twenty-nine. Hardwood storage is carried on here, though floating storage of hardwoods is now confined to the Surrey Commercial Docks. The buildings 10 and 11 represent perhaps the most modern development in the whole port. They are the objects of interest to all dock experts and present a dramatic contrast to the original 1 and 2 warehouses on the opposite side of the dock, the oldest dock warehouses in the port. In 10 and 11 there are new characteristics of transit shed design chiefly made necessary by the use of the fork lift truck in place of manual piling.

Mechanical handling on quays and in transit sheds has only been introduced into the Port of London since 1946; and because sheds 10 and 11 were the scene of pilot experiments, a brief digression on the subject is merited here. In the first place, equipment for a mechanical berth consists of 1,500 pallets. These are loading trays measuring six feet by four feet and can be picked up by the fork of a fork lift truck. Eyes welded at each corner of the pallet enable it to be lifted by quay crane or ship's purchase. In the sheds fork lift trucks can pile up to sixteen feet high with a great saving in floor space, which is generally precious in the Port of London. Efficient employment of these machines entails sheds twenty feet high, wide doors, and as few stanchions as possible so that truck operators have room to manœuvre. Old transit sheds are not easily adapted to these requirements.

The expenses of cargo handling are not much reduced by mechanization.[6] It costs about £40,000 to equip one berth with the necessary mobile cranes, fork lift trucks, and the 1,500 pallets.[7] There are, however, considerable indirect economies: loading times are cut by as much as 20%; and in some cases discharge may be carried out at a speed 40% faster than that of manual gangs. This saving represents an advantage to the shipowner who has a quicker turn-round of his ship, and to the port authority or quay renter who benefits from a more economical use of the berth.

These three-storey buildings, 10 and 11, are 432 feet long compared with, for example, sheds only 300 feet long on the north quay of the Royal Albert Dock. The length is the same as the length of berth required for a modern 10,000-ton vessel. Each ground floor is twenty-four feet six inches high, has a transit floor above, and the third storey supplies warehouse accommodation. This vertical development is one effect of the inability to expand much laterally in the old docks, especially in such a 'peninsular' area between two docks. The transit operations are essentially the discharge of general cargo, notably green fruit, and tomatoes are a speciality of the adjacent Canary Wharf transit shed which is privately operated.

A and the B sheds of the Export Dock still serve export berths. Export goods often consist of transport units ranging from private cars to bulldozers and excavators. These three sheds are too low and too narrow for efficient operation, but the difficulties of lateral expansion in the area between the two docks are obvious, despite the fact that an additional twenty-six feet has been gained by building a false quay out into the Import Dock on the south side. Another peninsula between the Export and South West India Docks is even narrower. Since there is room for only one set of sheds and one road on the peninsula, the road is a quayside one. Normally, ships are excluded from the south side of the Export Dock, because quayside congestion would result from gangs working back-to-back within one transit shed.

In the South West India Dock F and G take discharge of general cargoes. H serves an export berth. This berth was chosen for the pilot experiment in the mechanization of exports in the Port of London, because the height of the shed was suitable for the mechanical appliances, which are at present mobile cranes and fork lift trucks. O normally serves an import berth, and green fruit is often handled there mechanically, and N serves another mechanized export berth. M and L are sheds with warehouse accommodation at the rear. Sugar in bulk is unloaded to L shed ; K serves an export berth. This intermixture of import and export functions need cause no surprise. It is another manifestation of the flexibility of water transport and is encountered in the other dock systems.

The installations of the Millwall Docks present many contrasts. Perhaps the most celebrated feature is the Central Granary built at the beginning of the century to serve the grain trade, a characteristic trade of this dock since its early days. The capacity of this building of ten storeys is 24,000 tons, and this and other silos of the Millwall Docks are served by floating grain elevators as well as shore installations to speed ships' discharge.

Opposite the Central Granary are buildings partly used as warehouses, but K and the ground floor of M, a general warehouse, south of K, rebuilt since the war, serve export berths.

The small dry dock in the south-east corner of the Inner Dock is of historic interest. It was the first dry dock allowed to be incorporated in a London dock system. In the first part of the nineteenth century the vested interest of Thameside shipbuilders had prevented the necessary inclusion of a dry dock and ship repair base in the docks. By the time the Millwall Docks were opened in 1868, a dry dock could be included since shipbuilding on the Thames was dying away, never to recover. Among the chief causes of its disappearance were the high cost of labour on Thameside; distance from the deposits of coal and iron, the consumption of which increased markedly in the shipbuilding industry after 1850; high overheads near London; and the difficulties of launching into the tideway.[8] These adverse factors do not weigh so heavily against ship-repairing which is usefully situated close to the turn-round point of shipping; and the southeast corner of the Millwall Docks is one of the many areas where ship repair and maintenance can be carried out on dock premises.

West of the dry dock further evidence of the importance of the grain trade is displayed by the installations of Messrs. McDougalls Ltd. These have been erected on sites secured on long leases from the P.L.A., where the grain trade had previously been localized by the provision of primitive silos. In the south-western corner of the docks there are the premises of Messrs. Timber Wharves Ltd., the name proclaiming the function, where timber may be processed as well as stored and landed. A, B, C, D, and E serve both import and export berths.

Elsewhere around the Millwall Docks are many of the original buildings, very small in comparison with the modern installations. The modernization of the area south of Glengall Grove depends, amongst other things, upon whether the pedestrian bridge is to be maintained across the dock. If this were removed, a new berth might be made astride the present position of the bridge up the western side of the Inner Dock. This would lead to a redevelopment of the oldest dock buildings.

F

The East India Dock berths are confined to the north and east quays. The traffic to them is brought exclusively by vessels in the 'short-sea', or near-continental and coastwise trades and discharging and loading are carried on with the aid of 1½-ton cranes, though 3- and 5-ton cranes are now considered standard in seaport operations. The south and west side of the dock are due for reconstruction; at present old warehouses on the south quay store plywood and feeding stuffs. On the north side of the basin (see back endpaper) a very old warehouse, A, is used for the storage of sugar, plywood, and animal feeding stuffs, while the eastern quay serves as a base for wreck lighters of the P.L.A.

The chief characteristics of this dock system are the contrasts between ancient and modern; between the near-continental and coastwise berths on the one hand and the installations for ocean-going vessels from all continents, except South America, on the other. Storage is provided for certain goods such as grain, timber, and unrefined sugar; but general warehousing is not extensive. Goods are lightered here from the Royal Group of docks, and lightered hence to the London and St. Katharine Docks and river wharves. All these characteristics point to the fact that the India and Millwall Docks form the most representative dock system of the Port of London, combining features of dock systems both upstream and downstream where each feature is displayed on a wider scale.

Dock workers had to live near their work in the days before the internal combustion engine and the decasualization of labour. Two nuclei of their settlement in the formerly empty Isle of Dogs marshes were Millwall on the west and Cubitt Town on the east, the latter established in 1843 and named after Sir William Cubitt (1791–1863), co-founder of the present firm of builders. Until the coming of the omnibus, which travels the road following the curve of the meander from Limehouse to Blackwall, these people were remarkably isolated. Their social development became trapped between the docks and the riparian wharf and industrial front-ages.[9] Only in the Island Gardens, opposite Wren's Greenwich Hospital, is it possible to penetrate to the riverside. Many such areas isolated by dock premises are to be found in the Port of London. They are so distinct in character as to merit the term 'Dockland'. In fairness to the West India Dock excavators, it must be pointed out that the docks came first; but the development they set in motion was to provide an environment for their workers which was to cut them off from the rest of London. Even the East India Dock, small as it is, cuts off an area towards the Lea (*see* back endpaper). Fortunately, all inhabitants of this area have given way to the claims of wharves with frontages along the Lea meanders (Bow Creek). Slum clearance and war damage have eradicated the worst areas elsewhere. Moreover, the dock worker can now live further afield, if he chooses.

The Commercial Road with its extension, the East India Dock Road, and its tributary, the West India Dock Road, are, for this country, rare examples in recent times of roads cut with a Roman or Parisian ruthlessness across what was formerly a mass of east London streets. Before the coming of the docks these great arteries were not necessary. All heavy transport to and from the City was by water. There had been formerly a network of straggling villages, from Spitalfields to Poplar. Many of their old highways were superseded in importance by these 'commercial' roads, built in the period 1803–10. Poplar High Street, for example, is atrophied and no longer the social centre of the southern half of that borough—a role now assumed by the East India Dock Road. The Chinatown district of Limehouse had its centre in the West India Dock Road and its branching streets. The thriving colony with its 'touristic' oriental atmosphere has departed, but some Chinese remain and their restaurants are a notable feature of these streets. It seems apt that a service road to the docks should be the axis of the area settled by those who habitually offer services to people who come out of the main West India Dock gates.

## 2. LONDON AND ST. KATHARINE DOCKS (*see* front endpaper)

The Western Dock (without the jetty) of the London Docks and the Wapping Basin were the original works excavated following the approval of the London merchants' plan by Parliament in 1800. The dock was opened in 1805, and later were added the Eastern Dock (1828), Shadwell Old Basin (1831), and Shadwell New Basin (1858). St. Katharine Docks were independent of this system for thirty-six years after their opening in 1828–9.

The sponsors of the London Docks laid great stress on the advantage of the proposed situation, 'as near as may be to the City of London and the seat of commerce'. Unlike the Isle of Dogs marshes, the site was not entirely empty. At the end of the eighteenth century it was described as

> 'mostly an uncultivated waste, and much of the rest is laid out in gardens and gardeners' grounds; being intersected with but few straggling buildings; all of them small, some new, but mostly old, bad in condition and fame, and of little value. There is there already a vacant space unoccupied by any buildings, large enough for an extensive dock and warehouses of large dimensions upon pulling down a few straggling houses . . . and . . . the removal of a few inferior streets that are intersected with gardens and rope-walks.'[10]

When the St. Katharine Docks came to be excavated, this problem of pre-existing buildings was more serious. Twenty years had passed and the proposed dock site, though of only twenty-three acres, was adjacent to the City boundary. Over 1,100 houses were pulled down, and the Royal Hospital and Collegiate Church of St. Katharine were compensated by the grant of premises in Regent's Park, and were not reinstated in the East End, at Stepney Green, until 1948.

Again the Thames Ballast layer proved to be a great help in giving secure foundations for both series of docks. It runs as a fifteen-foot-thick stratum nine feet below O.D., overlying London Clay.

The principal entrance to the London Docks is the Shadwell Entrance to the Shadwell New Basin built in 1858; the entrance to the Shadwell Old Basin was dammed near the river in 1922. The Wapping Entrance was closed in 1956, and the Hermitage Entrance was closed as long ago as 1914 to form the site of a pumping station which raises the height of the water in the dock to fifteen feet two inches above O.D. Vessels of up to 330 feet in length (about 2,300 gross tons) can be locked at the present Shadwell entrance; the limiting factor is the sixty-foot beam restriction. However, by using the Shadwell Basin as a lock, vessels of up to about 2,500 tons can enter.

Today the chief disadvantages of the lay-out of the London Docks are: the discontinuity of the dock area, divided into three by public roads; the converse of this, namely, the necessity for three bascule bridges on these public roads which seriously interrupt road services to and from the quays on the south side; and the restrictions placed on extension of the dock space. This latter consideration applies in two dimensions: not only is it impossible to expand horizontally, because of built-up property adjacent to the dock wall; but also vertical expansion is difficult, because of the danger of overloading old quays, almost all of which are honeycombed by vaults.

Site restriction is at its worst in the St. Katharine Docks. Nevertheless, a remarkable length of quay was achieved by their designer, Thomas Telford. Less praiseworthy was the decision of the dock company's directors to open a dock in 1828 with an entrance lock suitable only for vessels of a size current at the end of the eighteenth century. This lock, which has never been widened, permitted entry only to vessels of about 1,000 tons. Nowadays, no ships use these docks; their warehouses are served by barges.

Because of the great importance of warehousing in this dock system, there follows a brief introductory digression on bonded warehouses (*see* also Chapter VI). Before the Warehousing Act of 1803, the duty which had to be paid on most imported cargoes was required by the Customs at the moment of entry into the country. As can be imagined, this procedure had crippling effects on the entrepot trade and warehousing. The Act of 1803 allowed importers of sugar and other West Indian products to lodge them in the warehouses of the West India Docks without payment of duty until their future sale. The merchants availing themselves of this procedure had to give a bond for the payment of double duties, subject to the single duty being paid within twelve months. The warehouses were secured by the joint locks of the Crown and the merchant. Subsequently, the warehouses of the London Dock became bonded warehouses for imports of rice, tobacco, wine, brandy, and geneva (with the exception of products from the East and West Indies). The advantages to trade and to the new docks were very great. Bonded warehouses were an important addition to the twenty-one-year trading monopolies which the first two dock systems had received.

The descriptive tour will begin with the installations of the Western London Dock, and proceed eastwards to the Eastern Dock and the Shadwell New Basin. Then the warehouses of the St. Katharine Docks will be described together with the associated Cutler Street Warehouses. Several of the dock warehouses of this system were severely damaged by air attack, and the map still shows great gaps in the Eastern Docks of both the London and St. Katharine Docks.

At the north-west corner of the Western Dock is the principal entrance to the London Docks, and the scenes from this viewpoint epitomize the dock characteristics. Outside the gates the narrow approaches via East Smithfield, Dock Street, and The Highway typify the constricted approaches to this dock system. Inside the entrance looms the great Crescent Warehouse, the centre of wool storage in the Port of London; and in front of it is the area where H.M. Customs wine gaugers are at work on hundreds of casks which are in the care of P.L.A. coopers. This view sums up the great importance of warehousing and of the ancillary services provided by the P.L.A. in these docks. Moreover, except where berths and sheds are rented, the actual functions of ship discharge are carried out by employees of the P.L.A. This is not the case in the other dock systems, except at the India Docks.

The major installations north of the Western Dock are four-fold: the northern line of warehouses; the central line of ware-houses; the quayside transit sheds; and the underground vaults.

Of the northern line of warehouses, the Crescent Warehouse is the chief place of wool storage and display for which, in four storeys, thirty acres of floor space are available. On the top floor buyers may inspect the bales by natural light from a glass roof, where about 80% of the wool passing through the dock ware-houses is displayed to private buyers. The New Warehouse (Marston Shed), adjacent to the Crescent, deals with Bordeaux wines. Next comes the line of six single-storey Pennington Street Warehouses, of which 1 and 2 have been converted into staff canteens. In 3 examination is carried out of wines delivered from 1-5 vaults beneath the quay; 4 and 5, Pennington Street are bonded stores for cased wines; and 6 is an iodine store.

The five four-storey central warehouses, opened in 1805, take delivery from the five north quay transit sheds and from barges bringing goods discharged from ships at other docks. The functions of these warehouses may be briefly noted : 1, rubber and general goods; 2, essential oils and drugs; 3, canned goods; 4, gums, waxes, and general goods; and 5, a general warehouse. The disadvantages of the older warehouses of this system are their inadequate cranes and the low load capacity of the floors.

The transit sheds (1912) receive deliveries on two floors from ships, lying at import berths, from Spain and France. Spanish exports are also dealt with at 5 shed.

It follows that there is a lot of cross traffic between warehouses and transit sheds across the road which has to serve the north quay. This leads to some congestion, for there is no room for a quayside road. Indeed, the visitor sees the following notice: *'Persons going from one part of the dock to another should use the roadways and paths at the back of the sheds. There is no thoroughfare along the quays.'* This is greatly in contrast with what has recently been suggested as the ideal requirements of a quay—namely, a width of thirty-six feet between quay wall and transit shed in order to provide a working space for transport.[11]

Under all the warehouses and some quays of the Western Dock are extensive vaults storing wines and spirits, with the heavy wines (ports and sherries) to be found in the Crescent Vaults and Nos. 1-5 vaults. Below warehouses and transit sheds a forest of stone pillars supports brick vaulting about eight feet high, and the whole labyrinth is ventilated by a system of tunnels. The temperature remains fairly constant, about 60°F, and this is of great value in maturing wines and spirits in casks.

North of the cutting to the Eastern Dock, A and B respectively store plywood and veneers; south of the cutting are two single-storey sheds where duty paid goods are warehoused. In F hazardous goods are stored. A great advantage of dock warehousing is the fact that owing to the great range of types of storage space available, similar classes of goods can be kept together. Such selective storage is granted a lower rate of fire insurance.

A new shed has been erected on the south-eastern side of the Western Dock, B shed Eastern Quay, and this, with C and 6, is used for goods to and from Italy. The opportunity has been grasped to provide a splendid road at the rear of this shed. Short-sea trades are served by berths on the western side of the Wapping

Basin and along the southern side of the dock. There are found the Gin Bottling Warehouse and the Cased Brandy Floors of the South Quay Warehouse, with the South Quay Bottling Vault (for wines) beneath.

Number 9 shed, Western Quay receives plywood and paper. Behind this, four- and five-storey warehouses, 7, 8, and 9, west of the Western Dock store wool, sugar, and general goods.

The jetty was rebuilt by the P.L.A. in 1914, on the site of a former wooden structure. On each side double-storey transit sheds serve berths for the coastal trade. A service road runs under cover in the centre of the jetty, and the tenants of the transit sheds usually provide their own transport for goods right through to their destination.

At the West Quay Shed, just to the north of the jetty, experimental shipments of wine in bulk have been received since 1953. The trade has continued but has not so far greatly expanded. Opposite the Crescent Warehouse, 6 Warehouse is a plywood store and is where duty-paid bottling of a famous French vermouth is carried out. The reasons why the bottling is carried out here instead of at Marseilles as formerly are the reduction in duty and the savings of freight charges when the vermouth is transported in bulk. The capacity of this bottling department is over 1,000 dozen bottles a day.

The reader will have seen what a remarkable dock this is, with manifold functions. In the simple account above over forty separate installations have been referred to.

The effects of war damage are particularly noticeable around the Eastern Dock. A reconstructed berth on the west quay is used by vessels in the Canada and Great Lakes trade, the only extra-European service from this dock system. Vaults in the north-western part of this dock are used as warehouses for general cargo —a novel proceeding which emphasizes the ample vault accommodation of the London Docks. The south-eastern part of Eastern Dock is a lying-up berth, while 10 warehouse, on the south-west, partly rebuilt with reinforced concrete, is a tea warehouse, and the basement is used by the expanding trade with Germany. When it was rebuilt, the old first floor was omitted, enabling a ground floor twenty feet high to receive mechanical handling apparatus.

Number 11 warehouse, west of the Shadwell Basin, is a general store for German and other cargo. An interesting new building is to be found on the north-west of this basin, 27 Berth. A two-storey brick transit shed has replaced four old single-storey sheds, 70 feet wide, 43 feet back from the quay. There was no possible expansion beyond a maximum quay and shed space of 133 feet, which is now used in a different way. The new building is 28 feet from the quay and 60 feet wide, thus allowing room for a service road, 45 feet wide, at the rear. This graphically illustrates the improvement in road accommodation needed around old premises, even at the cost of some quay space. In the north-eastern part of the basin Swedish and French trades are catered for.

In the St. Katharine Docks emphasis was placed on the provision of extensive warehousing facilities. To this end the great five-storey warehouses were built flush with the quay wall to avoid the transit shed operation. The omission of transit sheds is a saving if all the cargoes are the same; but if they are varied, the sorting has to be done on the warehouse floor, and this is costly.[12] In modern dock installations transit sheds are not omitted. These warehouses are supported by massive Greek columns to allow hand-truck movement along the quays. No other vehicle, except electric trucks, could penetrate the forest of columns and brick supports. Road approaches are narrow: a road 'tunnel' leads to B Warehouse, Western Dock, and the frowning bulk of A Warehouse looms around a tiny yard, overwhelming the horse-drawn drays of tea blenders waiting there.

C, Western Dock, is a five-storey warehouse for sugar, paper, and general goods. I, between the Western and Eastern Docks, is an international storage centre for ivory, and a general cargo warehouse. A and B are tea warehouses, with the vaults under B used to store vegetable oils.

The installations of the Eastern Dock suffered severely from bombing attacks. Of the four buildings which remain, one is the premises of the P.L.A. Civil and Mechanical Engineering Department; two, G and H, are tea warehouses, and there is a shed for storing matches.

In 1836 the St. Katharine Dock Company purchased the massive Cutler Street Warehouses from the East India Company, and they are now administered as part of the London and St. Katharine Dock system. These warehouses, between Middlesex Street ('Petticoat Lane') and Houndsditch, in the angle between the City wall and Liverpool Street Station, are one of the little-known wonders of London. They are five storeys high and cover five acres, with 600,000 square feet of floor space. Miraculously, they escaped damage during the aerial bombardment and are in amazingly fine repair considering that they were built in 1782.

An astounding variety of goods is stored here in this real-life treasure-house. The chief commodity, occupying over one hundred rooms, is carpets, from the finest Persian to the more stereotyped Indian. Often, over 100,000 'pieces', carpets and carpet materials, may be in the warehouse at one time. Nearly all the carpet factors of London, mostly Armenians, have their premises in the streets close by the international market in this warehouse. Isinglass, silks, ostrich feathers, and drugs of all kinds[13] are stored here. Made-up tobacco is inspected by H.M. Customs and warehoused. This includes all cigars and cigarettes imported into London. In the basement a bottling department is to be found. As many as 10,000 bottles of wine may be distributed from here daily. A post-war innovation is the storing of 350,000 bottles of vintage wines.

A further digression may be made here to note that, as the governing body of the port, the P.L.A. performs many services which are not strictly part of the port function. In the London and St. Katharine Docks some of these services are the sampling and display of wool, and the repair of wool bales and wine casks. At Cutler Street not only are wines bottled and binned but ostrich feathers are graded and playing cards banded.

Goods cannot flow freely from point of dispatch to reception by manufacturer or ultimate consumer for four major reasons: transhipment, pause for sorting, sale *en route*, and necessity for time to mature under experienced supervision. The first two operations obviously take place in the Port of London, the third will apply if London is the national or international market for the commodity, and the fourth will apply if the nature of the goods warrants it. All these varied causes imply an interruption to the flow of goods. This can be used to service the product in some way. Since dock premises include warehouses as well as docks, some of these services can most usefully be performed while still within the dock authority's responsibility.

During the last century dock labour was among the cheapest available and it was natural to use it for performing other services besides loading and unloading. The P.L.A. inherited the tradition of such a practice. This reason, rather than any tendency to 'vertical economic integration' between warehousing and manufacturing, lies behind the many operations which the P.L.A. is prepared to perform for importers.[14]

The chief characteristics of this dock system are the great range of warehouse accommodation available and the fact that of all its regular shipping lines only one crosses an ocean (the service from the Eastern London Dock to Canada and the U.S.A., via the Great Lakes). Considering the vast amount of goods in store and the relative smallness of the docks, it is not surprising to learn that half the cargoes are received by barge. There is no rail communication to these docks, and the road services suffer some congestion. However, the docks derive advantage from being surprisingly close to the heart of commercial London. The centre of the system is only a mile and a quarter from the Bank of England, and the group may be distinguished from all other docks of the Port of London by being called the 'Town Docks'.

The London and St. Katharine Docks are located in Stepney, a riverside metropolitan borough, the population of which once helped to provide the port's labour force as watermen and dockers, although there were always a number of small miscellaneous workshops just outside the City wall. This industrial variety has persisted, and the population is not now so dominated by port workers as it once was. It may be estimated that half the dockers employed in this system live outside Stepney.[15]

Great changes have resulted from the extensive war damage; and the post-war five-storey flats of the L.C.C. form great contrasts with the surviving low huddled buildings of the nineteenth and early twentieth centuries. These contrasts are well exemplified along the length of Cable Street from the industries at the eastern end near Commercial Road through post-war flats in the centre to a crowded Negro quarter along its old narrow western portion near the London Docks.

Shadwell and Wapping are two quarters largely eviscerated by the excavation of the docks. The fragments which remain form another of those areas isolated between the docks and riverside warehouses. Post-war flats have been erected east of the Western Dock, and the St. George in the East Hospital, until it closed down at the end of 1956, tended its patients just south of the Eastern Dock in surely one of the most insalubrious of situations for a hospital. Although the Metropolitan Line of the London Underground runs through Shadwell and Wapping, beneath the Eastern Dock, no buses serve the area south of the docks. There is no shopping centre, and all roads to the north and east may be interrupted by bascule bridges. As in the case of other dock systems, the London and St. Katharine Docks exert a depressing influence on the habitability of an area of considerable extent outside their boundaries.

A great human geographical contrast may be observed beneath the northern approach to Tower Bridge. Westwards is the promenade in front of the Tower of London. Here thousands of tourists bent on visiting the Tower take their ease between views of the Tower battlements and the Traitors' Gate on the one hand, and the river and Tower Bridge on the other. A Beefeater's information kiosk against the bridge is their eastern limit; for as the tourist thinks to move under the bridge he glimpses the canyon-like, lorry-ridden thoroughfare of St. Katharine's Way. On the south-east corner below Tower Bridge is a coffee-stall where dock workers may take a snack. The tourist blinks at the blackness of St. Katharine's Way; the docker stares back stolidly. The tourist goes back to the Tower, and one more visitor to London turns his back on its port.

This scene emphasizes the sharp contrasts to be observed between the functions of small areas near the centre of a large city. Nowhere are the contrasts in urban scenery so profound as in all directions from Tower Hill.

## REFERENCES

1. The Royal Albert Dock was a promotion of the London and St. Katharine Docks Company and was opened in 1880. The Tilbury Docks were opened by the East and West India Dock Company in 1886.

2. Below Trinity High Water (11·4 feet above O.D.) at centre of sill. Trinity High Water, a datum confined to the Port of London, varies in fact from 11·03 to 11·53 feet above O.D. because it was originally a mark made on the Hermitage Entrance Lock as long ago as 1800, as required in the Act for constructing the London Docks. A levelling by Trinity House in 1865 defined T.H.W. as being 12·5 feet above O.D. (Liverpool) which itself varies with regard to the later O.D. (Newlyn). See alphabetical list of references under T. E. Longfield (1932), W. B. Hall (1939) and J. W. Wooding (1943).

3. Reference to the index will elicit such general topics embedded in the text. The particulars of the docks given in this and the following chapter represent the situation in the early part of 1956. Detailed changes in dock operation continually occur, but now that the port is emerging from its post-war reconstruction phase, the general picture is likely to remain stable for some years.

4. W. B. R. King and K. P. Oakley, 'The Pleistocene Succession in the Lower Part of the Thames Valley', *Proceedings of the Prehistoric Society*, 2 (1936), 67.

5. Their principal locations are: Western Region, Brentford, Chelsea Depot; Southern Region, Nine Elms, Battersea, Blackfriars, Charlton, and Deptford.

6. There has been a similar experience at Liverpool.

7. The pallets do not leave the berth. 'Throughout-movement', when cargo remains on the pallet during its sea voyage and to its destination, awaits international agreement, or at least standardization at different ports.

8. S. Pollard, 'The Decline of Shipbuilding on the Thames', *Economic History Review*, III (1950), 72–89. The difficulties mentioned are well exemplified by the mishaps attending the launching of Brunel's *Great Eastern* at Millwall, an operation not finally achieved until 1858. This remarkable vessel of 18,915 gross tons was the largest ship in the world at that time and remains the largest ship ever built and launched on Thameside.

9. Millwall, a Third Division professional football club, moved from this area in 1910 and now plays south of the river at New Cross.

10. W. Vaughan, *On Wet Docks, Quays, and Warehouses for the Port of London, with Hints respecting Trade* (1793), 4–5.

11. *P.L.A. Monthly*, XXX (1955), 190.

12. Sir Joseph Broodbank, *History of the Port of London*, 2 vols. (O'Connor, 1921), 155.

13. Civet (perfume fixative), gum gamboge (water colour), aloes, vanilloes, mint, dried roots, and narcotics, including opium.

14. Now that dock labour is among the dearest manual labour available, it is to be expected that these operations performed by *dock labourers* may tend to diminish in scope and magnitude. Nevertheless, the general principle remains: 'working-up' of imported raw material (which includes vastly varied functions) is always most economically carried out as close as possible to the change from water to land transport.

15. Based on figures quoted by K. B. Pailing, *Planning Problems of London's Waterside Areas* (Unpublished thesis presented for the Diploma in Planning, 1952), 105. [Copy held at L.C.C., County Hall.]

# CHAPTER V

# TIMBER DOCKS AND DOCKS DOWNSTREAM

3. *Surrey Commercial Docks*
4. *The Royal Docks*
5. *Tilbury Docks*

3. SURREY COMMERCIAL DOCKS (*see* front endpaper)

THE heterogeneity of the docks which make up this system is a legacy of independent development, at one time by four separate companies. Cutting through the tangled web of history, it can be said, as an opening generalization, that the Grand Surrey Canal Company's area of operations was Russia Dock, Stave Dock, and Albion Dock; and the centre-piece of the Commercial Dock Company was the Greenland Dock, though it later acquired docks of companies it had absorbed to the north and south. The Canada Dock (1876) and Quebec Dock (1926) were constructed after the dock system had been unified, first under private control in 1864 and then under the P.L.A.

Between 1696 and 1703 the Howland Great Wet Dock, the first enclosed wet dock in the port, was built, 1,070 feet long, 500 feet wide, and 17 feet deep (*see* Chapter II, p. 46). In 1763 it was renamed the Greenland Dock when it became associated with the whaling trade. The Commercial Dock Company had acquired and improved it by 1810; but it was not thoroughly rebuilt until 1904. This operation entailed some difficulty, because the useful Thames Ballast stratum here lies over Thanet Sand instead of London Clay, and the preparation of quay foundations was subject to great delay. The splendid Greenland Dock quays are now split up by no less than six exits, four of which restrict the length of berths. The longest continuous length of quay in this dock is 800 feet despite a total quay length of 2,250 feet.

The Commercial Dock Company had taken over the South Dock (built in 1811 by the East Country Dock Company) in 1851 and had absorbed the docks, ponds, and yards to the north

95

belonging to the Baltic Dock Company which had begun operations in 1809.

On the other side of the system was the operational sphere of the Grand Surrey Canal Company. This Company had received its Act of Incorporation in 1801, with the object of constructing a canal from the Thames via Camberwell and Croydon to Epsom, in order to provide a transport artery for the growing needs of the metropolis in market-garden produce. This project proved a failure, and the canal never reached beyond Camberwell with a branch to Peckham. The Company, re-formed under the title of the Grand Surrey Docks and Canal Company in 1855, constructed the Albion Dock in 1860 and was amalgamated with the Commercial Dock Company in 1864.

Despite this great variety of origin, resulting in a seeming incoherent mixture of dock and quay with five separate depths of water, timber is the predominant cargo dealt with everywhere, except in the Greenland and South Docks. At the outset, the docks of this system were not designated as legal quays, and cargoes other than timber could be landed only under special sufferance.

Certain aspects of the timber trade need to be noted here: its seasonal nature; the fact that most London timber merchants have always had comparatively little storage capacity of their own; and the historic circumstance that directors of the dock companies which built up this dock system were often drawn from the ranks of timber merchants. These three facts have reacted upon one another to produce the present method of ship discharge in this trade.

The docks were developed for the storage of large quantities of timber. Ships could dump their cargoes, arriving as seasonal flushes, upon the quays, and the wood could then be sorted out to the various qualities and sizes and placed in piles ready for sale. Ships' gear was suitable for dumping timber on the quay, and the dock directors saw little need of providing cranes. To this day timber is discharged almost exclusively by means of ships' gear. This method has practical advantages, because, owing to the bulky nature of the cargo and its seasonal arrival, the tracks of any quayside cranes would quickly become blocked unless special and perhaps inconvenient measures were taken. It might be said that in the process of timber discharge the transit sorting operation, normally carried out in transit sheds, is carried out on the quays themselves; whereas the timber sheds actually have the functions of warehouses.

For many years an army of men was required to carry the sawn lumber from its position on the quay to its special pile in shed or timber yard. There were over 1,000 of these deal porters in 1939; now a little over 200 are available for the docks. The labour shortage in part accounts for this decline which has been made good by the use of mobile cranes. These have eliminated the need for men to carry the timber for considerable distances on their shoulders, as they formerly did by running along gangway planks.

From all this the modern requirements of a timber importing berth may be deduced. A quay about 24 feet wide is overhung by a shed roof to within about 6 feet of the water to allow ships' gear to operate. Movement along the quay is under cover with 16 feet of clearance from quayside to the shed stanchions and the built-in sides of the sheds. The interior of the shed should be 30 feet high to the eaves (compared with about 20 feet before 1940), with alleys 15 feet wide, laid with a 10- to 12½-foot width of concrete. These allow mobile cranes to pile up to 23 feet high to left and right. Modern sheds are built to these requirements, with 65-foot spans, allowing for 25 feet of storage on each side of the 15-foot alley.

In September 1940 these docks suffered the greatest damage of any single dock system. No less than 176 timber sheds were destroyed, mostly by fire, and 57 have had to be demolished since. The South Dock Entrance was destroyed, and much of the warehouse space and all the cold storage accommodation were razed. This put an end to the provision trade formerly handled at the Greenland Dock. These Greenland and South Docks will be left to the end in the detailed descriptive tour which follows.

The Surrey Entrance, almost opposite the principal entrance of the London Docks, was built in 1860, together with the basin. Since the dimensions of the entrance lock are small it is mainly used by barges and smaller timber vessels for only five to six hours per day tide.

The Stave, Lavender, and Lady Docks, of shallow depth, are only used by barges and for floated timber. The P.L.A. alone possesses about 130 barges and also employs those of lighterage

G

contractors. These barges are intended exclusively for internal lighterage, particularly to the northern yards of the dock system (Stave, Lavender, and Acorn Yard North, respectively west, north, and east of Lavender Dock) which are served by barges alone. No less than 500 barges are to be found within these docks during the timber season: one fifth of these enter or leave each day. The sheds at Stave, Lavender, and Acorn Yards have been rebuilt for piling by mobile cranes. Three modern sets of sheds at Acorn Yard North are the centre of undercover hardwood storage in this system.

Lady Dock is where floated timber is at present concentrated. There are several advantages of floating storage: economy, one man handling rafts weighing hundreds of tons; some woods develop cracks if stored in the open air, especially mahogany and rock-elm; and water soaks out unwanted sap fluids which might take a long time to evaporate. In Lady Dock the predominant floating wood is Douglas Fir for cutting into planks.

Russia Dock is the only one of this north-eastern series which receives ships. These are limited to a draught of seventeen feet because the authorized depth of this dock is only nineteen feet.

Quebec, Albion, and Canada Docks receive vessels via the Canada–Greenland cutting and the Greenland Entrance. There are no berths on the eastern side of Quebec Dock which has a shelving bank. Timber sheds for Albion Dock (Centre Yard North) were built in 1954 and the Albion Yard development plan is proceeding (1956) with the erection of fourteen new timber sheds.

Of the 40,000 standards[1] of timber now stored at these docks, compared with 80,000 in 1939, only 32,000 standards of softwood can be stored under cover, in addition to 15,500 tons of hardwood. Only about 20% of the imported timber arriving in the Surrey Commercial Docks is handed to the P.L.A. for storage; the remainder is discharged into barges for landing at other waterside premises on the river and the canals.

The Canada–Greenland cutting is in process of being widened. It was built 27 feet deep nearly 100 years ago, and, like most old cuts, it was invert, the sides sloping inwards. This was satisfactory for the hulls of sailing ships, but vessels are now square-built so that the effective depth is only 23½ feet for vessels up to 420 feet long. The result has been that the largest vessels laden with timber have been compelled to lie at berths in the Greenland Dock designed to deal with general cargo, because timber ships from British Columbia are as big as 10,000 gross registered tons. The cutting is in process of being widened from 60 feet to 82 feet, giving an effective width of 80 feet at the bottom for vessels up to 450 feet long. The new side-wall will be made vertical to a depth of 31 feet 6 inches. This operation, which will open up three docks to much larger vessels, should be completed in 1958.

Norway Dock is an engineering base. There is a repair yard here, the headquarters of the P.L.A. Marine Engineering, and the depot of Messrs. Harland and Wolff, contractors to the P.L.A. for all floating plant.

In the north-west part of the Greenland Dock area, 14 stores plywood, piled to the roof and delivered to road transport as required by fork lift trucks. Sheds 11 and 10 are used for transit purposes for goods delivered by barge from vessels lying in Canada, Albion, and Quebec Docks. The ships which berth here maintain the only regular passenger service between London and Russia, via Leningrad. Three berths in the north-eastern part of Greenland Dock are appropriated to shipping lines running to North America. A small building in the north-eastern corner of the dock area provides storage for hardwoods.

North of the Greenland Dock Entrance, 3 and 4 (with 1 and 2 to the north, to be rebuilt) are used for plywood storage. South of the dock entrance, 15 is a regular discharging and loading berth for vessels from Finland. At the rear, 2 is used for sorting and temporarily accommodating import goods before their delivery to barges in the South Dock. Import goods are stacked on pallets by fork lift trucks. Adjacent on the west is 8, a new transit shed with a ground floor enabling export goods to be piled mechanically eighteen feet high on pallets. Import goods are dealt with on the upper floor which has a verandah on each side. On the Greenland Dock side goods are delivered to the verandah; on the South Dock side these goods are shipped off to barges. A shipping line runs to this berth from India and Pakistan.

In the south-western part of the dock at 12 is a berth for a liner service carrying general export and import goods to and from Canada. At the western end of the dock, 12a, rebuilt in 1955, is mainly used for general cargo from barges, which has been transhipped from vessels in the Canada and Greenland Docks.

The South Dock Entrance has been closed so that vessels are received via the Greenland–South Dock cutting, the greatest limiting factor here being a restriction on vessels' length to 240 feet. South of the dock, 1 and 3 are four-storey warehouses, which survived the war, and store general cargoes, as well as giving transit accommodation to a line regularly plying between Hamburg and London. No. 4 shed, at the western end of this dock, also receives general cargoes from the continent. The Railway Yard is leased to timber merchants for storage.

The chief characteristics of this dock system are, firstly, the concentration of specialized timber berths where no quayside cranes are to be found since unloading is by ships' gear. Discharge into barge is very important; 80% of the timber is received into barges. There are buoy berths in the centre of the timber-discharging docks where *all* timber is discharged to barges. The second major characteristic is the change to general cargo berths south of Redriff Road. There are fourteen general cargo berths in this system, compared with thirty-six timber berths. The former, it has been shown, are for the most part appropriated to medium-sized vessels of shipping lines running to certain countries.

The contrast between the docks north and south of Redriff Road is a result of the dock company's decision in 1893 to rebuild the Greenland Dock for general cargo in order to take advantage of the relatively short haul to central London. This contrast of function might be guessed at from the lay-outs shown on the map. The Greenland and South Docks, despite their combined water area, have less yard space than, for example, the much smaller Albion Dock. All the buildings south of Redriff Road are set back a little from the quay to allow room for quayside cranes to deal with general cargo. North of Redriff Road the ground plan shows that sheds are almost flush with the quay walls at timber berths (though a new general cargo berth is being constructed on the south-east of Canada Dock for Finnish traffic).

There is the usual cut-off area of housing adjacent to this system. Here it takes the form of a ribbon development along Rotherhithe Street which runs parallel with the meander curve of the river from Limehouse Reach to the Lower Pool. East and north of this road are the premises of riverfront wharfingers; across the street the boundary wall of the Surrey Commercial Docks everywhere presses close.

4. THE ROYAL DOCKS (*see* back endpaper)

Of the 117 deep-sea berths in the five dock systems of the Port of London, fifty-three are to be found in the Royal Docks, accommodating ships generally in the range between 10,000 and 30,000 gross tons. Everything here is on a much larger scale than in the docks upstream. A walk along all the quays would entail a journey of ten miles. The map shows that this system follows the modern trend of dock design, which may be described as 'simple lineal quayage'. The only peninsular area is to be found between the Royal Albert and King George V Docks.

In 1855 the Victoria (*sic*) Dock was opened by the Victoria Dock Company and was the first dock in the port with main line railway connections. It was taken over by the London and St. Katharine Docks Company in 1864 in order to improve their facilities, because the average size of vessels had by then risen to 2,500 tons. The flood-plain site had been bought for little more than its agricultural value. Two hundred acres of this land to the south were left vacant as potential pasture land for cattle; this livestock trade did not materialize. Simple lineal quayage was not then a feature of the dock; eight jetties projected from the north quay, and the south quay was interrupted by a pontoon dock where ships could be overhauled and repaired.

1880 was the year when the Royal Albert Dock was opened, and at this time the prefix 'Royal' was added to the name of the Victoria Dock. The new dock was built to deal with traffic from even larger ships which could not at that time enter the Royal Victoria Dock. It was equipped with single-storey transit sheds, and there were no warehouses. These are characteristics which it retains to this day. The Lower Gallions Entrance was built in 1886 in order to compete with the Tilbury Dock being built by the East and West India Dock Company. It was damaged during the war and was not reopened until 1956.[2] During the interim all vessels were received via the entrance to the King George V Dock.

The King George V Dock was part of the 1910 improvement

plan of Sir Frederick Palmer, first chief engineer of the P.L.A.[3] The dock was opened for traffic in 1921 and repeats the pattern of the Royal Albert Dock, except that on the north side six double-storey brick transit sheds were built and on the south a series of seven dolphins (jetties parallel to the quay) was installed.

The Thames Ballast stratum, 20 feet thick, is present in the Royal Docks area, descending from 7 to 20 feet below O.D. from west to east. It overlies first London Clay and then Chalk in the same direction. In the eastern docks it has proved its worth as a foundation. When the Royal Victoria Dock was constructed, the ballast was removed in a mistaken idea that it was permeable, and puddle clay was substituted, 'a remedy far worse than the disease'.[4]

The descriptive tour begins at the western entrance of the Royal Victoria Dock. Since the construction of the Silvertown Way this entrance has been used only by barges; and the western end of the water area which was formerly a tidal basin has now been incorporated in the dock. There is no disadvantage in receiving vessels through the other docks: it is easier to navigate in the still water of docks with no dangers from river traffic; and the western entrance of the Royal Victoria Dock always involved a difficult turn in the river.

Z shed and berth were built in 1926 for the reception of chilled meat when 35 shed (Royal Albert Dock, western end) proved too small to serve vessels in this trade. Over three-quarters of the arrivals consist of chilled beef, with some frozen lamb and offal.[5] Bananas and some fresh fruit and butter are also handled direct at this meat berth, but some of the fruit and butter, and all other goods are handled through F shed.

Eastwards, the projection of the north quay wall shows how the quay space has been extended into the former water area. The warehouses X, W, M (six storeys), and T and V were all once on the waterside. These (excluding X) and the line of shell warehouses behind are the tobacco warehouses of the Royal Victoria Dock. The Tobacco Department of this dock also administers the Commercial Road Depot (see front endpaper). This warehouse was originally designed to serve Tilbury Docks, but since tobacco is the chief commodity in store, the building has temporarily become a functional adjunct of the Royal Docks.

The splendid new north quay, three quarters of a mile long, was completed as recently as 1944 with five brick and concrete transit sheds and warehouses, 500 feet by 150 feet. Older transit sheds are much shorter than this. The top two storeys of these buildings warehouse tobacco for the most part; the ground floors serve as transit sheds. F serves an unallocated berth, but of course it is always occupied, often with meat, fruit, and general cargo from South America, notably from the Argentine; E is rented to a Canadian line for exports and imports; D is rented to a United States line for exports and imports; C deals with exports to the Far East; and B serves the berth of inward Australian and New Zealand services.

Shed A was designed in 1927 as a second berth to deal with South American chilled meat. Chilled beef again predominates. Loading platforms, some specially equipped for the mechanical discharge and delivery of bananas, are seen extending to the rear. Citrus fruits, tomatoes, and other general cargo are landed via the Orange Shed, adjacent on the east.

The south side of the dock was progressively remodelled after the disastrous Silvertown explosion of January 1917 when many of the pre-existing sheds were wrecked. One silo was destroyed and others damaged. Yet those silos started a grain tradition, and private millers have erected huge installations here, with accommodation for 114,000 tons of grain unloaded by suction; they are the tenants of the P.L.A.

The digitate shape of the Pontoon Dock is an interesting survival. This bears witness to the first attempt to provide ship-repairing facilities in the docks of the port. Ships were dry-docked here by means of pontoons or shoring for repair and overhaul. To the south is a large yard with a quay rented to a timber merchant.

In the south-west of the dock, 3, 2, and 1 sheds are used for exports and imports, particularly from the Americas and the West Indies. The upper floor of 2, part of 3, and the top two floors of 1 store tobacco. Behind these buildings are the corrugated iron sheds numbered 5 to 8 used as warehouses because they are some distance from water: 5 and 7 store general cargo, 6 is really defunct, and 8 now houses tidal models of the Thames.

The lay-out of the Royal Albert Dock is simple but gigantic. To the west of the north quay, which has an uninterrupted straight length of over a mile, is 35 shed with 5 Cold Store behind. As was noted above, 35 shed originally served a chilled meat berth. With the increase in the size of meat vessels and the construction of larger berths in the Royal Victoria Dock, this berth and shed became available for other cargo. Yet because it was an open shed with an iron roof, it was not suited to dealing with general cargo and was developed in 1938 to give shelter for the specialized landing of bananas. Vessels in the Jamaican trade carry about 160,000 stems. Half of these can be landed in one day.

Number 5 Cold Store has accommodation for 140,000 carcasses of beef, lamb, and mutton ; and 6 Cold Store (1918) can hold 302,000. In 1920 three transit sheds, 29, 31, and 33 were replaced by two brick-built sheds designated 29 and 33, sheds, with a continuous upper floor equipped as a cold sorting floor for meat ; but recently this has been in use as a cold store at 16°F. for 198,000 carcasses,[6] though the chambers are rather large for freezing. Nowadays, the sorting of meat is done on the quay which cuts down the number of times it is handled.

A short digression on the methods of ship discharge, especially in these docks, is appropriate here. Whereas in the India, London, and St. Katharine Docks the P.L.A. has the sole right of discharging ships, in the Royal Docks (as at the Surrey, Millwall, and Tilbury Docks) discharge of cargo is carried out by shipowners or their stevedoring contractors. The methods of discharge may be considered under three headings: 'quay conditions', 'overside conditions', and 'wharf conditions'.

The shipowner may rent a transit shed from the P.L.A. under a Quay and Shed Space Agreement. This enables him to land his cargo into the rented shed for sorting to Bill of Lading marks and quantities for subsequent delivery to barge or land transport. In the latter case the shipping company performs the quay work on behalf of the P.L.A. Such are 'quay conditions' of discharge. These conditions are very common in the Royal Docks, where the principal shipping lines have their appropriated berths.

'Overside conditions' are where the shipping company's responsibility ceases at the ship's rail. The P.L.A. then undertakes all quay work.

'Wharf conditions' apply when the shipping company undertakes all operations at berths rented on long-term agreements.

There are at present no such berths in the Royal Docks because elsewhere they are usually let to coastal or short-sea traders, like the steamer wharves in the river; hence the expression 'wharf conditions'.

All the other quayside buildings around the Royal Albert Dock are transit sheds. They were built 336 feet long so that at the time they were designed one shed would serve one berth. Now, the increased average length of vessels using this dock is about 450 to 550 feet and results in the inconvenient arrangement of one and a half sheds per berth. Nearly all are export berths with the exception of 29 to 33, beneath the 7 Cold Store, which receive New Zealand goods, and 15 shed. Sheds 25 and 27 have been converted for use as fully mechanized berths serving the New Zealand export trade. At the western end of the dock are the dry docks which, with the King George V dry dock, make up the largest area of ship repair in the port.

The King George V Dock embodies the same general pattern as the Royal Albert Dock though it opened forty-one years later; but there are modifications which were made necessary by the increase in the size of shipping during that period. The transit sheds are longer, varying from 500 to 550 feet. On the north side the sheds are built in pairs in three long brick buildings which provide extensive warehouse space on the upper floor for tobacco. The original intention was to provide two transit sheds one above the other, but only one set of ground outlets was provided for each pair of floors. Ideally, each transit shed needs its own approach road and three rail tracks behind: a shed track, a waiting track, and a running track. Duplication of these services could not be provided particularly because of the restricted nature of the peninsular area between the docks. The top floors of these buildings now function as tobacco warehouses.

The south quay pattern demonstrates explicitly the importance of the barge traffic. The seven dolphins, each 520 feet long, were installed thirty-two feet from the quay so that a ship can discharge either direct to the quay or to barges lying inside the dolphin or outside the vessel. The idea seems ingenious, and while there is no question of removing the dolphins, it is open to doubt whether they are as effective in promoting flexibility of discharge as they appear. Along other quays similar results are achieved by berthing ships against dummies; quayside cranes are then not restricted to their own dolphins, and, if required, ships can work to and from the quay with their derricks. The interior clear height of five sheds on the south side of the King George V Dock was raised from ten feet to fourteen feet six inches, an effect of the requirements of mechanical handling appliances.

This descriptive tour of the Royal Docks may be concluded with reference to some practical aspects of dealing with modern ocean-going vessels. It is a common occurrence to have 12,000 tons of general cargo for discharge. Transit sheds are chock-full during unloading. On the other hand, export cargoes are usually made up of large quantities of manufactured goods in small lots. Import cargo has to be stowed according to Bill of Lading quantities and descriptions; export cargo has to be stowed according to ports of discharge. Import and export traffic therefore require different handling techniques, and for the largest vessels it is most economic if they are not dealt with at the same berth. If London is the terminal port during these operations, the ship's officers go on leave and the crew are paid off; the ship may also proceed to dry dock. Otherwise, the ship goes on to discharge or load part cargoes 'up the coast', an expression which includes near-continental ports.

G. A. Wilson (1953), 564, has shown how much space is necessary for road traffic serving export berths. Firstly, it is assumed that of the twelve berths on the north side of the Royal Albert Dock only three would be loading at full speed of 500 tons of cargo per day. Let it be supposed that the 1,500 tons of cargo are all brought by road (in practice about 20% comes by rail, and cargo can be collected in transit sheds before loading begins into the ship). Since vehicles do not always arrive fully laden, about 500 lorries would be needed, and, assuming a length of thirty feet per vehicle, a double line of 500 vehicles, one and a half miles in length, would be necessary, exceeding the length of the twelve berths by half a mile and greatly impeding the access to the remaining nine berths.

Three further aspects of the landward communications of the Royal Docks should be mentioned. Firstly, north of the Royal Victoria Dock are the Royal Victoria Exchange Sidings, the largest of their kind in the country.[7] They are divided into three groups, outwards (10 roads accommodating 369 wagons), reception (11 roads, 464 wagons), and shunting and marshalling (10 roads, 367 wagons). To the reception group every day come about twenty-two trains of mixed export loads and empty wagons. After being marshalled, these are hauled by some of the score of P.L.A. locomotives to the appropriate quays of the three docks on which the wagons will be further re-shunted to the rear of the sheds where they are required. Wagons carrying, or destined to carry, heavy or low-rate goods (*e.g.* steel billets, earthenware piping, or cumbersome cargoes) are often run in front of the sheds along the quayside. At 12 noon and again at 5 p.m. six to ten trains containing special and perishable cargo may make for the outward group of the Exchange Sidings and each is divided and re-marshalled to perhaps eight outward trains, in addition to those worked forward throughout the day.

Secondly, passengers to or from liners leaving or entering these docks may be embarked or disembarked there or at the Tilbury passenger landing stage, according to the wishes of the shipping company. Mobile customs arrangements and other passengers' facilities can be transferred to the berth in question. Passenger trains vary in number per week; one week there may be four, during the next only one. Liverpool Street Station, for the Royal Docks, or St. Pancras Station, for Tilbury Docks, are used in preference to the nearer Fenchurch Street Station, because the latter has few facilities to deal with passengers' baggage.

Thirdly, the *Royal and Other Docks Approaches (Improvements) Act*, 1929, brought into being a twentieth century counterpart of the specially constructed dock approach roads of over a century earlier.[8] This is Silvertown Way which sweeps in a graceful arc from the Barking Road to Silvertown (*see* back endpaper) and caused the closure of the western entrance of the Royal Victoria Dock, except to the passage of dumb barges. The old road pattern, including the former dock road, is truncated on either side of this great highway which had another beneficial result in ventilating a former slum area. The dwellings of 3,600 people were demolished, and they were rehoused in an estate in West Ham. At the same time a new bridge over Bow Creek (River Lea) relieved an east London bottleneck.

There is the usual remnant residential area, cut off between the docks and the developed riverside. Silvertown takes its name from Messrs. S. W. Silver and Co. (*cf.* Cubitt Town, Isle of Dogs), a firm of Cornhill outfitters who, in 1852, transferred their water-proofing works at Greenwich to this stretch of the riverfront. The North Woolwich Railway, branching from the Eastern Counties Railway at Stratford, reached the river in 1847. With the opening of the Victoria Dock in 1855, industrial activity grew apace. The riverside plants of Woolwich Reach include three cable works (North Woolwich and Woolwich), two soap works, flour mills, and two great sugar refineries.

The banks of Woolwich Reach are intermediate in character between the continuous general cargo wharves upstream and the less continuous wharves serving larger riverside units which characterize Lower Thameside (*see* Chapters VI and VII).


5. TILBURY DOCKS (*see* back endpaper)

The Tilbury Docks were opened in 1886 by the East and West India Dock Company to meet competition from the Royal Albert Dock opened in 1880. By the choice of a situation so far down river (the original dock entrance is twenty-six miles downstream from London Bridge), the sponsors of this dock system hoped to reap the benefit of a water situation at the gateway of the port. At the period when the docks were opened the river traffic was becoming embarrassed by shallows in many of the reaches (*see* pages 65–6). Tilbury has rather short river approaches, and at the time the docks were opened only one area of shoals in the Lower Hope Reach had to be navigated. To overcome the disadvantage of the land situation, which was the long distance from London, the docks were designed for rail transit; no warehouses were built, and, until 1939, the system was virtually isolated as far as road transport was concerned.

For a time the docks were a costly failure. This was chiefly due to the disadvantages of the site which resulted in expensive excavation in the deep spongy alluvium, since, not surprisingly, the river deposits thicken downstream. The Buried Channel stratum (Thames Ballast) was found at an average of forty feet below O.D., overlain by very soft mud and clay with layers of peat.[9] This depth is over twice as great as in the case of the Royal

Albert Dock. The difficulties of construction led to a change of contractor, costly litigation upon this change, and the resultant increase in construction expenses to £1·7 million above the £1·1 million estimate. The difficulty of reaching a stable foundation is a subsidiary reason why no multi-storey warehouses are found in Tilbury today. Heavy buildings would require elaborate foundations adding greatly to their expense. Even a light structure such as the wooden-floored transit shed 4a, built in 1912, had by 1955 shown settlement in the floor varying from one foot to four feet six inches due to subsidence caused by differential shrinkage of the alluvium.

Instead, warehousing facilities were provided in London at the Commercial Road Depot (*see* front endpaper) which the dock company leased from the rail company. This depot has passed into the hands of the P.L.A., but is now administered by the superintendent of the Royal Docks.

The original dock system consisted of the three branch docks leading to a basin entrance lock and a tidal basin. The diagonal orientation of these docks north-west to south-east was probably due to the fact that the land purchased by the dock company lay to the south-west of the railway of the London, Tilbury and Southend line, which had arrived at the riverside in 1850 to serve the ferry to Gravesend. Choice of point of entry from the river and the decision to provide a Tidal Basin were influenced by the desire to obtain the calmest water at the entrance to the docks. Along the north bank of Gravesend Reach there is slacker water, since it is on the inside of a meander, and the Tidal Basin served to remove the actual dock entrance to a sheltered position away from the tidal stream of the river.

This design has proved to be a mistake. The Tidal Basin has increased the area of slack water to such an extent that it is a great mud trap and one of the worst areas of silting in the port (*see* page 67). Moreover, the Basin entrance lock proved incapable of being easily extended, so that when the western entrance lock was constructed in 1929, a new orientation had to be found opening westwards into the Northfleet Hope. This is the largest dock entrance in the port, 1,000 feet long and 110 feet wide.

The Branch Docks were constructed with dimensions comparable to those of the Alexandra Dock, Liverpool, 200-300 feet wide. However, Merseyside Docks are not so encumbered by barges, and the Branch Docks are now rather too narrow for the most efficient movement of ships and barges. In addition, there need scarcely be a reminder of the disadvantages of peninsular quay areas which cannot be expanded.

The transit sheds of the Branch Docks deal with both export and import cargoes. At the head of the West Branch Dock is a novel feature. A shipping line operates a transport ferry service using converted ex-Government tank landing ships (in the 4,000-ton gross class), and wheeled vehicles are driven down ramps which were cut in the quay during the build-up for the Normandy invasion. A regular weekly service is maintained between Tilbury and Antwerp for the carriage of laden road transport vehicles.[10] Up to seventy heavy commercial lorries can be stowed. There are several advantages in this type of transport, whereby laden vehicles run right through from door-to-door, which offset the cost of carrying the land vehicle across the sea : the service is speedy, since there are no delays in handling at the ports ; packaging is cut down to a minimum, or in some instances entirely eliminated ; and the absence of handling virtually cuts out the risks of breakage and pilferage. The service is also particularly convenient for the export of automobiles and railway rolling stock ; and all military vehicles destined for the British Army in Germany are transported in this way.

The largest vessels now regularly using the port are dealt with at the three splendid berths in the Main Dock, which was extended in 1917 westwards from the Basin entrance lock at right angles to the original system. As far as possible these Main Dock berths follow the principle of simple lineal quayage. Here has taken place one of the largest of the post Second World War improvements of the P.L.A. This work was made necessary by the increase in the size of liners using these docks. Since 1954 the P. & O. and Orient Lines have added three vessels to their respective fleets near the 30,000-ton class with a length of over 700 feet. In 1956 the Orient Line ordered a vessel of 40,000 tons, and early in 1957 the P. & O. Line ordered another of 45,000 tons, 814 feet long. Both ships are intended for the Australia route where these lines operate jointly. New port installations must be provided in advance of the entering into service of such new vessels.

A new berth, 842 feet long, has been recently constructed in the north-west area of the Main Dock, with a T-shaped transit shed 532 feet long. Concrete monoliths have been sunk fifty to sixty feet to reach gravel. The construction of the new berth has involved cutting back 310 feet of the west quay of the West Branch Dock (and the incidental obliteration of a possible site for Number 1 Transit Shed). By the end of 1956, when the scheme was completed, a second berth with a 400-foot transit shed had been constructed on the site of the former 2 and 3 sheds on the west side of the West Branch Dock. The width of the western part of the Main Dock has been increased to 900 feet, thereby allowing easier manœuvring for large vessels on the east side of the West Branch Dock at 7 and 8 sheds.

On the south side, the dry dock, constructed in 1928, 750 feet long, is the largest in the port. West of this, four berths are available for the largest vessels, the fourth berth being at the western end of the Main Dock. The transit sheds serving these berths have an average length of 600 feet, about twice the length of the older sheds of the Branch Docks. At all these berths there is a forty-two feet six inches depth of water.

Coaster-type vessels use the original entrance, but the traffic there consists mainly of barges. The usual 'free water' clause was inserted into the Act approving construction of these docks. Promoters of the dock expected that the downstream situation would give rail transport unapproachable advantages over water transport for carriage of goods to the upstream warehouses. This proved a vain hope. As much import traffic proceeds overside into barges as in the other docks. Half the exports are delivered by barge.

Only one small line running to near-continental ports has a berth in the Tidal Basin. From 1927 to 1932 a cross-Channel service, Tilbury to Dunkirk, was run from the Basin. Passengers from the north avoided travelling via two termini in London. Yet this service was withdrawn, a victim of a general law in rail–sea passenger transport : assuming that the total time and the total money spent on the journey is the same, passengers will prefer the route which gives the shortest sea passage, and the area of

England for which the Tilbury–Dunkirk route provided the quickest service was obviously quite small.

Overseas passengers arriving in the port may be landed at the Floating Landing Stage, opened in 1930. Ships may come alongside at any state of the tide and then proceed to their berths in Tilbury or the upper docks. However, should the shipping company desire it, time can be saved by taking the passengers into the dock. The same alternatives are available for the embarkation of passengers. Close to the Landing Stage is the Baggage Hall, the only building specially constructed for the use of sea passengers in the whole port. From Tilbury Docks rail passengers usually arrive in London at St. Pancras.

The Cargo Jetty, a magnificent double-decked structure 1,000 feet long, dating from 1921, is not so much used as one might think, principally because of the disadvantages of berthing a large modern ship in a tidal river (see page 45). A recent development (1956) is that ships pause at the jetty to discharge natural rubber latex by a 325-foot pipe-line to seven storage tanks (with a total capacity of 100,000 gallons), sited on the south-west of the Main Dock. Vessels may then complete the discharge of their other cargo in the docks.

One of the most interesting developments at Tilbury has been the change in the land traffic. When the docks were opened, there could be no road haulage to London, and railway traffic continued to be predominant until 1939. Since 1946 a great change has occurred.

TABLE XI

*Land Traffic to and from Tilbury Docks*

|  | Year ended March 31, 1939 Tons | Year ended March 31, 1956 Tons |
|---|---|---|
| Exports delivered by : |  |  |
| Road    ...    ...    ... | 17,774 | 202,790 |
| Rail    ...    ...    ... | 69,925 | 98,084 |
| Imports conveyed by : |  |  |
| Road    ...    ...    ... | 9,912 | 113,732 |
| Rail    ...    ...    ... | 130,359 | 64,103 |

The figures may be interpreted quite simply. For comparative purposes, let the loads of rail traffic to and from Tilbury in the year ended March 31, 1939, be represented as 100. Proportionally, road traffic in the same year was 14; rail traffic in the year ended March 31, 1956, was only 81, but during the same year road traffic soared to 158.

This dramatic increase in road transport has been achieved only by a change in dock lay-out. For example, in the seventy-six feet between 16 and 17 sheds, *i.e.* between the Centre and East Branch Docks, there was no road, but five rail tracks. One of these tracks has now been removed, another moved closer to the shed, and a roadway twenty-three feet wide serves the peninsula. Before 1939 the only road was that across the western entrance to the south side of the Main Dock. Since 1939 one and a quarter miles of road have been provided. Quays, loading banks, and alleys to sheds have had to be widened, and many outbuildings have had to be removed to provide enough parking spaces for vehicles.

Table XI also illustrates the great increase in total trade at Tilbury. This is because the larger and longer the general cargo liners become, the more certain it is that the largest and longest vessels will be handled at the new berths provided at Tilbury. Tilbury is not an outport of London, as Bremerhaven is of Bremen, Cuxhaven of Hamburg, or Cherbourg and Le Havre are of Rouen and Paris.[11] This dock system might have developed as an outport if it had not been incorporated in the Port of London in 1909. The P.L.A. would then have been driven to providing the large berths required by shipping further upstream, possibly in a new dock north of the Royal Albert Dock, at great cost, to which would have been added the expense of a longer deeper river channel of approach. The wisdom of instituting a unifying authority for the whole river is apparent. The result is that the outports of London are not found on the Thames but in more suitable situations on the Essex and Channel coasts.

To the north-west of the docks, 340 acres of marshland are available for future development. This helps to convey the impression of rural isolation at Tilbury compared with other dock systems. Built-up areas do not press so close to the dock boundary. Alone of London's five dock systems, Tilbury was not seriously

H

damaged during the war: its single-storey sheds and large open spaces gave incendiary bombs little opportunity to start big fires; moreover, it is probable that the enemy desired to spare Tilbury for future use as a major pierhead for the invasion of this country.[12]

The chief characteristics of the functions of the docks are the provision of berths for the largest vessels regularly using the port, with old-established connections with Australia, New Zealand, and India, and the fact that all the cargoes are in transit.

The names of Tilbury and Gravesend are often linked as if they referred to twin settlements on the threshold of the port. Nothing could be further from the truth. Gravesend grew up as a lateral river port on a Chalk bluff (Deptford, Greenwich, Woolwich, Erith, and Greenhithe have similar sites). In Gravesend Reach sailing vessels waited to navigate upstream with the tide or for a favourable wind to proceed out to sea. From here the 'Long Ferry' to London operated from about the thirteenth century until the introduction of a mail coach service, 'a comment on the bad roads'.[13] The situation of Gravesend within the port is still significant: it is the headquarters of the London Pilotage Service where river and sea pilots exchange duties.

The 'Short Ferry' across the river served Essex, but there was no riparian settlement on the marshes opposite. A housing estate was not erected there until the excavation of the docks in the late nineteenth century, and then dock workers made up the population of Tilbury, the only large-scale settlement on the alluvium of Lower Thameside. It has had to pay for occupying such a site, being affected by subsidence and also by serious flooding such as last occurred in 1953. There is no heart to Tilbury except the docks and no road focus; the chief roads lead to the landing stage and the ferry across to Gravesend.

## REFERENCES

1. A standard is 165 cubic feet, about two and a half tons of timber.

2. The five-year programme of reconstruction is described by J. A. Fisher, 'Reconstruction of the Gallions Lower Entrance Lock

at the Royal Docks of the Port of London Authority', *Proceedings of the Institution of Civil Engineers*, 5 (1956), 136–69.

3. His plan also included a new dock north of the Royal Albert Dock on 126 acres of flood-plain still owned by the P.L.A. This 'Queen Elizabeth II Dock?' may yet make a quartet of the Royal Docks within the next decade.

4. W. P. Shepherd-Baron, 'The Docks of London', *Proceedings of the Institution of Civil Engineers*, 3 (1954), 15 and 23.

5. The chilled meat trade built up again to these proportions after the final cessation of bulk buying of frozen meat during 1955.

6. A more accurate, but perhaps less graphic, method of giving the dimensions of cold stores is to quote their storage capacity in cubic feet: Number 5 Cold Store, 673,874 cubic feet; Number 6, 1,157,684; and Number 7, 956,233.

7. T. B. Peacock, *P.L.A. Railways* (Locomotive Publishing, 1952), 48–53.

8. D. Kennedy and H. E. Aldington, 'Royal Docks Approaches Improvement, London', *Journal of the Institution of Civil Engineers*, 2 (1935–6), 4–48.

9. The maximum depth of the foundations is no less than seventy feet below quay level.

10. The same shipping line operates a similar service between Preston and Northern Ireland (Belfast and Larne).

11. N. J. G. Pounds, 'Port and Outport in North-west Europe', *Geographical Journal*, CIX (1947), 216–28.

12. *P.L.A. Monthly*, XXIX (1954), 26.

13. L. R. Jones, *The Geography of London River* (Methuen, 1931), 24.

# CHAPTER VI

# RIVER TRAFFIC AND RIVERSIDE WHARVES

THE dock systems, extensive as they appear, are by no means the whole Port of London. In the decade 1947 to 1956 only just under half the net tonnage of shipping entering the port, or just under a third of the number of ships, found a berth in one of the five dock systems; and only about one-seventh of the tonnage of imports and exports actually passed over the quays of the docks (1953–4). This may seem to be an astonishing state of affairs, and it is the task of this chapter to explain how it is brought about.

Towards the end of the eighteenth century when plans for wet docks were approaching realization, the vested interests of the wharfingers, the Master Lightermen (*i.e.* the owners of river craft), and the Watermen's Company were among the principal opponents. They feared that their business and profession would suffer greatly owing to the diversion of traffic to the wet docks. To propitiate such opposition the following clause was inserted in the *West India Dock Act* of 1799 as Section 138.[1]

'Provided always and be it enacted that this Act shall not extend to charge with the said rate or duty of six shillings and eight pence per ton hereinbefore granted any lighters or craft entering into the said docks or basins or cuts to convey, deliver, discharge or receive ballast or goods to or from on board any ship or ships, vessel or vessels.'

This free water clause has had a far-reaching effect on the port. The first infant dock companies could grant such a considerable concession because they were each endowed with twenty-one-year trade monopolies in certain commodities and equipped with the rare privilege of bonded warehouses. Moreover, at the beginning of the nineteenth century, merchants preferred the greater security of dock premises. This period of 'protection' for the wet docks did not last.

116

The trading monopolies expired and were not renewed. With the development of a freer trade policy after 1860 a lesser number of goods became subject to import duty, giving more opportunities to private wharfingers with premises not previously bonded by H.M. Customs. As trade increased in the nineteenth century, so the docks faced increasing competition. The free water clause was embodied in every dock Act; and dock company directors watched their dividends shrink as every day the barges entered and left their docks, without hindrance, without charge, despite many appeals.

Upon the inception of the P.L.A., the free water concession, vital to riverside premises, was not omitted. Its latest expression is to be found in Section 68 of the *Port of London (Consolidtion) Act*, 1920:

'All lighters and craft entering into the docks basins locks or cuts of the Port Authority to discharge or receive ballast or goods to or from on board of any vessel lying therein shall be exempt from the payment of any rates so long as the lighter or craft shall be bona fide engaged in so discharging or receiving the ballast or goods . . .'[2]

The free water clause has permitted private wharfingers to compete or co-exist with both the dock companies and the P.L.A. The instrument that they have used to take advantage of the concession has been London's barge fleet.

RIVER TRAFFIC

The barge fleet is one of the most important and original features of the port. The Thames is not only a 'highway' of approach for sea-going vessels steaming to their destinations, but also a 'street', used by the internal tug-towed traffic of the port. To a landsman this great Port of London seems to be sprawled over an enormous area; to a lighterman it appears that all the port functions are carried out where his element, the waters of the river, can carry him no further.

Those concerned with lighterage inherit a long tradition. The foundation of the Watermen's Company was provided for in an

Act of Parliament in 1556. Watermen were distinguished from lightermen because they were concerned in the conveyance of passengers in wherries and rowing boats; lightermen were those working lighters and barges transporting merchandise. In 1700 another Act incorporated watermen and lightermen in one Company. After this date the two trades had dissimilar fortunes: the watermen's business declined because of the construction of bridges during the eighteenth century and the coming of the steamship upon the river (1818); the business of the lightermen increased parallel with the increase in the port's trade.

The present make-up of London's tug and barge fleet may be compared with the pre-war position.

TABLE XII

*London's Tug and Barge Fleet*

|  | 1936[3] | 1956 |
|---|---|---|
| Tugs: | | |
| Steam    ...    ...    ...    ... | 190 | 100 |
| Motor    ...    ...    ...    ... | 160 | 300 |
| Total Tugs    ...    ...    ... | 350 | 400 |
| Barges: | | |
| Insulated    ...    ...    ...    ... | 180 | 130 |
| Tank    ...    ...    ...    ... | 330 | 360 |
| Canal    ...    ...    ...    ... | 430 | 200 |
| Sailing    ...    ...    ...    ... | 430 | 15 |
| Mechanically propelled    ...    ... | 70 | 150 |
| Dumb    ...    ...    ...    ... | 7,440 | 6,130 |
| Miscellaneous    ...    ...    ... | 30 | —— |
| Total Barges    ...    ...    ... | 8,910 | 6,985 |
| Total Craft (Tugs and Barges)    ... | 9,260 | 7,385 |

Motor tugs are displacing steam tugs because they are more economical to operate. A steam tug must always have its fires burning; even during the week-end the fires must be banked in order to get away promptly first thing on Monday morning. A motor tug is easily shut down.

Comparing 1936 and 1956, the number of tugs had increased

by 14%, chiefly because of the increased traffic and changes in the working conditions of crews. The increased traffic concerned is not only that of the lighterage trade but of the port generally, since those tugs of highest power are engaged solely in attendance on liners, tankers, and ocean-going ships. The number of barges in 1956 was 22% below that of the 1936 figure. This has been brought about by wartime losses. Nevertheless, the increase in the average size of barges, from a burden tonnage of 112 in 1936 to about 150 in 1956 has resulted in a total carrying capacity for the barge fleet of about 5% greater than pre-war.

Insulated barges are used to carry chilled or frozen meat. Tank barges transport petroleum and take part in one of the longest regular hauls, from the Sea Reach oil refineries to the depots of west London. Canal barges have reduced dimensions to suit canal locks, especially on the Lea Navigation and Grand Junction Canals. The eclipse of the sailing barges is almost at hand. Most of the mechanically propelled barges are employed in trading to the Medway. They would not qualify as lighters granted free entry to the docks. Moreover, if such craft were used in the Thames lighterage trade, their motors would be lying idle for long periods, since the time during which a Thames barge is moving is only about a tenth of its total turn-round.

Consequently, most Port of London barges are 'dumb', without an engine. They are swim-ended, allowing a run of water fore and aft, which makes them more easily controllable when towed by a tug. Barges which were ship-shaped would have their projecting stem rudders often damaged when being towed or moored in the open river. Moreover, the protection given by the reinforced swim ends would be lost. Flat bottoms enable the barges to sit on the mud at low tide. There is normally one hold, which is hatched over for cargoes needing protection from the weather or which are dutiable and require to be placed under a Customs Officer's seal.

An idea of the tremendous movement of barges (Table XIII) is given on page 120. Under a P.L.A. bye-law up to six loaded barges may be towed by one tug, usually with the assistance of the tide. Normally, the Master Lighterman allows five days for transit after his barge has been placed in position for loading, made up as follows: two days for loading, one day for transit,

TABLE XIII

*Number of Barges Entered inwards at P.L.A. Docks*[4]

(Year Ended March 31, 1956)

| Dock System | Empty | Loaded |
|---|---|---|
| India and Millwall ... ... | 13,315 | 6,606 |
| London and St. Katharine ... | 3,824 | 3,522 |
| Surrey Commercial ... ... | 14,653 | 3,483 |
| Royal Docks ... ... ... | 20,483 | 12,964 |
| Tilbury ... ... ... ... | 6,629 | 2,644 |

and two days for discharge. After this period demurrage is usually chargeable.

This fleet of internal carriers within the port permits the great flexibility in discharge and loading that C. L. Wheble (1939) has usefully summarized :[5]

### Import Goods

A. Goods discharged ex ships and landed on the dock or wharf:
   1. For delivery to the dock or warehouse.
   2. For delivery to road transport for conveyance to local or inland consignee.
   3. For delivery to British Railways for conveyance to an inland consignee.

B. Goods delivered overside into barges:
   1. For delivery to specialized dock warehouses.
   2. For delivery to up-town warehouses with riverside premises.
   3. For delivery to sea-going or coastal ships for transhipment.
   4. For delivery to railway wharves for conveyance inland by rail transport.
   5. For delivery to industrial plants with waterside premises along the banks of rivers, canals, or inland navigations.

A similar set of eight different types of freight movement, in reverse, applies to the export trade.

This great variety of routes within the port is surely a wonderful asset, and C. L. Wheble has rightly pointed out that the lighterage trade is not an anachronism supported merely by an obsolete legal quibble of the free water clause.[6]

Suppose all barges were required to pay dock dues. The Master Lightermen would have to pass this cost on to their customers by means of higher lighterage rates. The customers would naturally protest at having to pay a price which included two sums for dock dues, first for the ship, then for the barge. The P.L.A. would most likely find itself obliged to lower its dues so that it received approximately the same revenue from a larger number of ship and barge movements.

If the abandonment of the free water clause would lead to little change in the total freight movement costs via lighters, would the saving in freight movement costs, via land transport be cheaper? Theoretically, the answer is yes. In effect, the dues paid on lighters entering the dock would slightly subsidize land traffic.[7]

Undoubtedly, more goods would be landed on the dock quays, driving the 'marginal' lighterage traffic out of business. Yet, under present conditions, land traffic at the docks is working to near capacity, and diversion of large amounts of cargo from the river would increase congestion and send up the cost. If all lighters were driven from the river, the same dock dues as now would be levied on vessels, and the dock quays would be scenes of unworkable congestion. In short, the lighterage trade is an integral part of the port, and should it cease, through a labour strike for instance, the port would be completely dislocated.

One specialized aspect of the river traffic deserves separate mention: the coal trade.

## SEA COAL

The sea coal trade to London is very ancient. As early as the beginning of the seventeenth century there were 200 colliers each supplying London with an average cargo of 73 tons per voyage. By the end of the eighteenth century about a million tons of sea coal kept London warm every year. L. R. Jones (1931) has explained the reasons why most of the coal came from the Northumberland and Durham coalfields.[8] There was the shortest of land haulages to the Tyne from the shallow seams which out-cropped close to that river. Before the days of rail transport coal could only travel long distances by water. In the last years of the eighteenth century the coal trade had so developed that colliers made up three-fifths of the tonnage of coastwise vessels entering London. These colliers were one of the chief causes of congestion in the port at that time (*see* page 40).

By 1850 London was receiving 3·6 million tons of sea coal per annum from 1,200 sailing colliers; but by 1865 the traffic was entirely carried by steam vessels. Railway haulage of coal had begun in 1845, and from 1865 until 1913 rail-borne coal tonnages every year were about the same as the tonnages of coal brought by the colliers. For fourteen years after 1913 rail-hauled coal exceeded the amount brought by sea, but since 1927 sea coal has again predominated.[9]

Table XIV analyses the sea-borne coal shipments to London since 1946. In 1948 and 1954 this represented 60% and 66% of the total coal consumed in the 'London Division' of the Ministry of Fuel and Power.[10] Some sea coal goes by water direct to industry, notably to Messrs. Ford Motor Company's coke ovens, and some to coal distributors; but during the period 1951 to 1955 inclusive, power stations consumed 27% of the total coal imported by sea, and gas works used 35%.

Thameside power stations and gas works receive coal at their own jetties from their own fleets of vessels, though extra colliers are regularly chartered. The fleets may be divided into two classes of vessel.

The 23 'down river' ships are of the normal design associated with coasting colliers, with a carrying capacity of 2,000-4,500 tons (6 to power stations, 17 to gas works). Gas works and power stations on navigable waterways in the London area receive coal which has been transhipped into barges from these down river vessels.

The 47 'up river' ships have carrying capacities ranging from 1,700 to 2,800 tons (24 to power stations, 23 to gas works). These are the largest vessels using the Upper Tidal Thames. They are popularly known as 'flat-irons' or 'flatties' because each has a low superstructure in order to navigate the arches of the numerous bridges. The funnel can be lowered (or is dispensed

TABLE XIV

*Shipments of Coal to London*

Coastwise Total (tons)

| From— | Bristol Channel Ports | North-Eastern Ports | Humber Ports | East Scotland Ports | Other East Coast Ports | Foreign[11] | Total (tons) |
|---|---|---|---|---|---|---|---|
| 1946 | ... | ... | ... | ... | ... | 13,642,242 | |
| 1947 | ... | ... | ... | ... | ... | 15,442,517 | |
| 1948 | ... | ... | ... | ... | ... | 15,138,570 | |
| 1949 | ... | ... | ... | ... | ... | 15,867,052 | |
| 1950 | ... | ... | ... | ... | ... | 16,522,264 | |
| 1951 | 1,151,717 | 14,589,286 | 1,336,395 | 319,729 | — | 222,499 | 17,619,626 |
| 1952 | 1,106,421 | 14,154,675 | 1,999,498 | 363,022 | — | 104,262 | 17,727,878 |
| 1953 | 1,131,545 | 13,571,333 | 2,898,211 | 411,841 | 1,450 | 301,089 | 18,315,469 |
| 1954 | 1,035,603 | 12,458,435 | 2,977,225 | 300,648 | — | 1,312,462 | 18,084,373 |
| 1955 | 750,402 | 11,879,581 | 1,297,402 | 275,658 | 2,950 | 5,412,113 | 19,618,206 |

with altogether in the modern diesel ship), and the masts are telescopic. Great skill is required in navigation. For example, when a vessel of 18-foot draught bound up river for Wandsworth Gas Works passes under London Bridge, the depth of water at the jetties of the gas works would fall short by three feet. During the passage upstream, with the river at a level low enough to negotiate safely beneath the bridges, the flood tide has provided sufficient depth of water at Wandsworth.

The 70-80 colliers of the public utilities account for about 60% of the coal coming into the Port of London every year. With about fifty other vessels, they are the modern carriers of the historic coastwise coal trade to London.

Two factors are coming into operation to challenge the dominance of sea coal as a provider of London's gas and electricity. Firstly, fuel oil and its by-products, notably from the Thames Estuary oil refineries, are to be used in increasing quantities in both gas and electricity undertakings in London.[12] Secondly, the completion of the super grid calls for the establishment of the future largest generating stations not on Thameside near the market, but in the valley of the Middle Trent near the low-cost inland coalfields with expanding production.[13]

BONDED WAREHOUSES

Just as few wharves could function without the lighterage traffic, so few of their associated warehouses could function without the bonding privileges conferred on them by H.M. Customs. In Chapter II it was shown that long before the excavation of wet docks, imported goods were landed at the Legal Quays owned by private interests for storage in the merchants' warehouses. About 1750 the functions of the wharf owner and warehouse keeper began to be combined in one person—the public wharfinger.[14] These wharfingers survived the advent of the docks and flourish today in many specialized forms. Indeed, the functions of riverside wharves vary considerably along different reaches of the river. In the first place, the account will be confined to the historical background of those riverside premises granted bonded facilities by H.M. Customs.

The merchant's bond given to the Crown for the future payment of duties solves a dilemma which all ports face. It is this. When imports are made which are liable to duty, it is natural to expect that the duty shall be levied at the point of entry into the country. However, if this rule were to be rigidly carried out, a merchant would be obliged to have always at hand a large amount of capital to meet the duty. In order to recoup his customs payments he might be forced to sell his goods immediately, perhaps on a glutted market. No great stock of goods of the same type could be built up for comparative display and sale.

One of the precepts of Adam Smith is relevant here:

'Every tax ought to be levied at the time, or in the manner in which it is most likely to be convenient for the contributor to pay it.'[15]

Two devices have been used to meet this principle as far as import duties are concerned. Firstly, in European and American ports free zones or foreign-trade zones have been set up.[16] Into these carefully guarded areas goods may be imported, operated upon, and re-exported without any payment of duty, provided they do not physically cross the boundary of the free zone. In the United Kingdom, however, another device is used: goods are placed in premises secured by the joint locks of the Crown and the merchant, such premises being known as bonded warehouses.

The free zone idea has two great advantages; for goods re-exported there need be no customs formalities or attendance; and the merchant has more freedom in which to operate upon his goods if he desires. However, the zone confers a monopoly privilege on its isolated area. It is often difficult to find such an area compact enough to fulfil all the functions required and equipped with a continuous and easily guarded frontier. This difficulty applies especially in London where the dispersed nature of the facilities of the port is apparent. A more material fact which killed the idea of establishing a free zone in London was the decision in 1909 to allow the public wharfingers along the river to remain outside the jurisdiction of the P.L.A.[17] Manifestly, a free zone in London would confer a special privilege on *either* the P.L.A. *or* the wharfingers; two free zones, one each operated by public and private interests, could not be made so equal that there would be no ground for complaint that one had greater privileges than the other.

The bonded warehouse system has been preferred and is used widely in the port. Goods may be placed in these warehouses duty-free and thence re-exported duty-free. Where duty has been paid on re-exported goods, customs drawback restores practically all the duty. Direct transhipments are duty-free.

Bonding is an ancient practice within the port and can be traced long before the so-called first *Warehousing Act* of 1803. The place where dutiable goods had to be landed, namely, the Legal Quays, was designated as early as 1558. The manner of the payment of the duty became important when the imposts grew in amount and scope.

The third and fourth Acts of James II, 1685, were concerned in raising supplies for repairs and stores for the Navy and the Ordnance and other of His Majesty's 'weighty and important occasions'. In the *Act for granting His Majesty an Imposition upon all Wines and Vinegar, imported between June 24, 1685 and June 24, 1693*, the importer had to pay the duty upon the landing of his goods or to be bound for payment in three equal instalments within nine months. The following act was an *Act for granting His Majesty an Imposition upon all Tobacco and Sugar, imported between June 24, 1685 and June 24, 1693*, and a brief edited extract is quoted below:

> '. . . every Merchant and Importer . . . after Entry of his or their Goods . . . shall become bound unto his Majesty with one or more sufficient Sureties, . . . in such Sums of Money as shall amount to the Value of the Duties hereby imposed upon his or their Goods . . . in case he shall not sell or export the same before the Expiration of eighteen Months from the Importation thereof, that he will pay all and every Duties imposed by this Act . . .'

These Acts, extended beyond 1693 by later statutes, were concerned in providing regulations for the merchants' bond; an *Act for encouraging the Tobacco Trade*, 1714, was concerned with a more permanent arrangement for storing duty-free goods. Section V of this Act is of great historic interest.

'And whereas several Merchants and other Persons concerned in the Importation of Tobacco of the English Planta-
tions, are frequently under Difficulties, and unable to give
good and sufficient Security for the Payment of the several
Duties imposed thereon : And whereas putting the same into
proper Warehouses may not only be an Ease and Convenience
to the Importers thereof, but also a Security to Her Majesty's
Revenue, Be it therefore enacted by the Authority aforesaid
. . . in case any Person importing any of the said Tobacco . . .
and shall then desire to have the said Tobacco put into
Warehouses, under the Queen's and Merchant's locks . . . it
shall and may be lawful . . . upon the Merchant's giving his
own Bond for the Payment of the Duties at the end of fifteen
months . . .'

Rum, coffee and cocoa, and rice were allowed similar bonded
warehousing facilities under Acts in 1742, 1767, and 1797 respectively. It has been pointed out that these facilities were intended
to favour the export trade.[18] The 1803 *Warehousing Act* extended
the privileges to many goods destined for home consumption,
provided that they were landed in the newly constructed wet
docks.[19] Although this Act was regarded as experimental, in 1805
the Treasury was granted authority to extend the bonding
privileges.

The 1803 Act conferred great privileges on the wet docks
compared with the riverside wharfingers, though the 1832 Act
subsequently allowed the Commissioners of Customs wide dis-
cretion in appointing sufferance wharves. Bonding privileges
became temporarily less important with the advent of free trade.
In 1842 there were 1,052 goods liable to import duty ; in 1860
there were only 48. In this era many of the modern public wharfinger firms began. Sir Joseph Broodbank (1921) has pointed out
that the dock companies were somewhat impersonal and con-
servative ; the wharves had the great benefit of being operated by
their owners.[20]

Enormously assisted by the fact that barges serving them
could enter the docks without payment of dues, the wharfingers
maintained their share in the expanding trade of the port. In 1889
there was a *Dock and Wharf Produce Agreement* on rates made

between the wharfingers and the Joint Committee of the dock companies. The former were allowed to charge 10 to 12½% less for the storage of many goods to offset the higher rates of insurance necessary for riverside premises.

Sufferance Wharves Acts and other legislation since 1832 have extended bonding privileges so that today nearly 170 firms, members of the two London wharfinger associations, have bonded accommodation. The majority of these public wharfingers deal principally with food imports. Since 1916 most of the public wharfingers have maintained agreed minimum rates with the P.L.A. The cost of lighterage, where necessary, is borne by the wharfinger since there is, in the main, one rate in the port for each class of goods. Of the two rates which wharfingers charge, *consolidated* (landing, warehousing, piling, re-delivery, and free rent for two weeks) and *immediate delivery* (unloading and immediate delivery to van), they naturally prefer the former type of business.

RIVERSIDE WHARVES[21] UPSTREAM OF LONDON BRIDGE

A comprehensive survey has demonstrated the high proportion (88%) of the industrial and commercial frontage of the Thames, within the County of London, which depends on river transport, or is 'linked' to the river. This proportion falls considerably on the Lea and the canals.

TABLE XV

*Proportion of Waterside Industrial and Commercial Frontage Linked to River or Canal (within the County of London)*[22]

|  | % |
|---|---|
| Thames ... ... ... ... ... ... ... | 88 |
| Lea and Stort Navigation ... ... ... | 77 |
| Limehouse Cut ... ... ... ... ... ... | 62 |
| Surrey Canal ... ... ... ... ... ... | 56 |
| Hertford Union (joins River Lea to Grand Union) ... | 47 |
| Grand Union (Regent's Canal) ... ... ... | 33 |

On the banks of the Lea, south of Hackney Marshes, Limehouse Cut (*see* front endpaper), and the eastern two miles of the Grand Union (Regent's Canal), more than 60% of the industrial frontages depend on water transport. Such frontages might be considered as ramifications of the Port of London. Perhaps the remaining waterside sites in the County of London are best regarded as being served by inland waterways branching laterally from the Thames. In view of this it is understandable that the concentration here will be on Thameside frontages.

As a prelude, the following table is quoted from information given in an official review.

TABLE XVI

*Numbers of Wharves on the Tidal Thames*[23]

| | |
|---|---|
| Privately owned public wharves (164 owned by 120 public wharfingers)    ...    ...    ...    ...    ... | 314 |
| Private wharves, other than those of gas, electricity, and water undertakings (owned by 182 undertakings) ...    ...    ...    ...    ...    ... | 234 |
| Wharves of gas, electricity, and water undertakings (16 for sea-going vessels): | |
|     Gas Works ...    ...    ...    ...    ...    8 ⎫ | |
|     Electricity Power Stations ...    ...    ...    13 ⎪ | |
|     British Transport Commission    ...    ...    2 ⎬    25 | |
|     Metropolitan Water Board    ...    ...    1 ⎪ | |
|     London Hydraulic Power Company    ...    1 ⎭ | |
| Coal wharves (13 for sea-going vessels)    ...    ... | 29 |
| Oil wharves (11 for sea-going vessels) ...    ...    ... | 37 |
|        Total    ...    ...    ...    ...    ...    ... | 639 |

Next, sixty-six miles of the waterfront of the Upper Tidal Thames and London River are considered, *i.e.*, both banks of the Thames from six miles above London Bridge to twenty-seven below the bridge in Gravesend Reach. Within these limits there are about 570 riverside wharves, and Figure 7 attempts a simple functional classification of them.

Firstly, two categories of wharf were distinguished according to whether the wharves deal with general cargo in packaged form or as separate parcels (predominantly foodstuffs); or whether the goods were landed in bulk (including grain, sugar, timber, and industrial raw materials). Secondly, five further categories were recognized according to the function of the premises served

I

by more specialized wharves. The resultant patterns are shown in the diagram.[24]

Despite the simple nature of the wharf classification, five patterns emerge. They are summarized below and will be discussed proceeding downstream.

TABLE XVII

*Patterns of Thameside Wharves*

| | LOCATION | |
|---|---|---|
| | North (*or left*) Bank | South (*or right*) Bank |
| *Nature of Pattern* | *Mileage above London Bridge* | |
| I. Widely spaced bulk wharves, with wharves serving public utilities ... ... ... ... | 14 — 2½ | 7½ — 2½ |
| | ¾ — bridge | 1¼ — bridge |
| II. General wharves, with some bulk wharves ... ... ... | *Mileage below London Bridge* | |
| | bridge — 2¾ | bridge — 2 |
| III.[25] Bulk wharves, with general wharves interspersed ... ... | 2¾ — 6 | 2 — 6 |
| IV. Bulk wharves, with wharves serving river traffic ... ... | 6 — 10 | 6 — 10 |
| V. Widely spaced bulk wharves and wharves serving public utilities, with wide intervals alternately on each bank of the river ... | 10 — 27 | 10 — 27 |

*Pattern I* is found on the north bank as far west as the river Brent, fourteen miles above London Bridge; but on the south bank there are few wharves upstream of Putney Bridge, only seven and a half miles above London Bridge. For the sake of compression, merely the downstream portion of this pattern from six miles above London Bridge is shown on the diagram (Figure 7). Wharves handling heavy goods predominate in *Pattern I*. Grain in bulk, iron and steel, non-ferrous metals, timber, and marble and other building materials are typical of the goods handled. An important feature is the number of wharves dealing with oil; no less than fourteen are to be found in this part of the Upper Tidal Thames. Six wharves serve gas works, and four serve power stations. Since this handling of heavy, dirty, or dangerous goods abuts on the recreational riverside, notably at Kew Gardens and

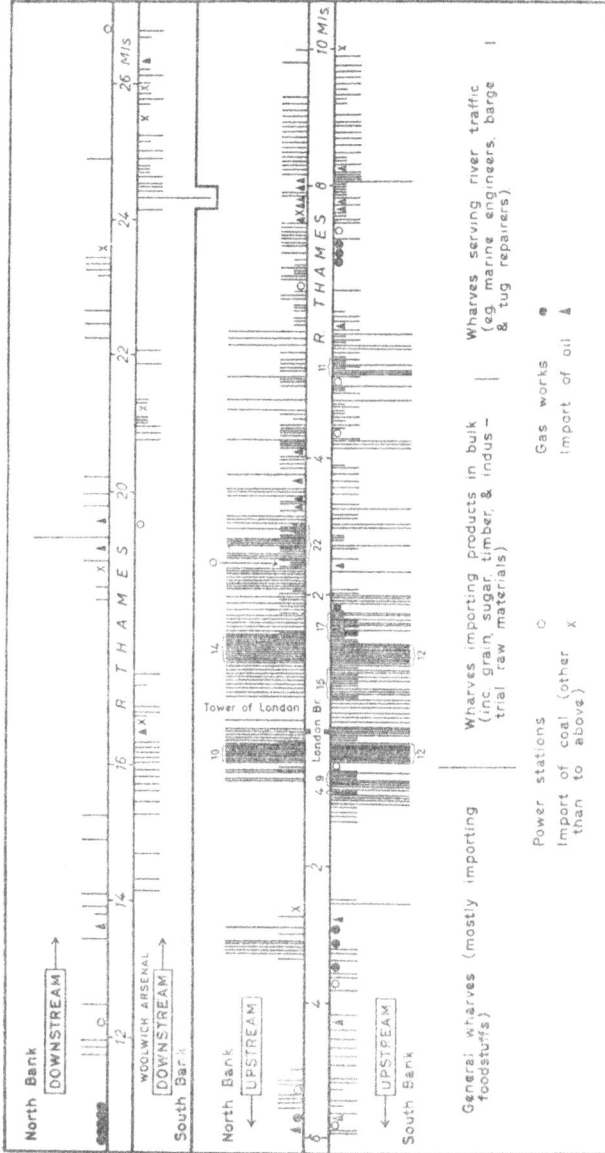

FIG. 7.—River Thames Wharves shown schematically according to Seven Types of Function. Mileage along the river is measured upstream and downstream from London Bridge.

near Richmond, the contrasts on the river banks are unusually sharp. Planning problems are acute.

West of Putney, on the south bank, the port function is limited by the installations of the West Middlesex Waterworks which occupy the curve of the Barnes meander. Downstream, as well as upstream, *Pattern I* is artificially limited; one might say, 'Rightly so!' The Chelsea and Victoria Embankments, with Millbank between, make significant gaps in the wharves on the north bank; the Albert Embankment and the South Bank sites form a complementary boundary on the south. The traditional view of London showing the Houses of Parliament from across the river is thus a very untypical 'un-commercial' view of the tidal Thames. Yet this same view will almost certainly show some of the port's dumb barges moored in the river. These are a reminder of the river traffic to wharves both east and west of those areas where London has found it desirable to give up the commercial use of the riverside. That commercial and industrial users of the river would occupy the sites thus denied to them is surely apparent from the sharp boundaries of the diagram. Indeed, many former traces of the features of *Pattern I* had to be cleared away before the nineteenth century embankments could be laid out. For example, queues of coal wagons were to be found in the lateral streets leading down from the Strand to riverside wharves.

An exception may be noted within this pattern. Just west of Vauxhall Bridge, on the north bank about three miles upstream of London Bridge, there are seven general wharves developed by the same firm since 1925. These are the only wharves within *Pattern I* specializing in the handling of foodstuffs such as fresh fruit and vegetables. Samples are delivered to importing merchants at the various fruit markets, including Covent Garden, Borough, Spitalfields, and Kew. The goods are then sold for delivery to buyers *direct* from the wharves. Bearing in mind the unusual westerly situation of these general wharves it will be seen that inland traffic avoids the congestion at markets and in central London. Most of the produce arrives by barge from ships in the lower docks. If merchants want parcels delivered at the market, they can avoid the delay of waiting perhaps all day at the docks for the landing of their goods from within a ship's general cargo. In addition, small Dutch coasters carrying onions, potatoes, and tomatoes may be discharged. This example has been singled out because the success of these wharves has depended largely on the fact that in recent years the Thames has been the least congested main street across London.

*Pattern II* begins a little upstream of London Bridge where the riverside is made up of general wharves dealing with foodstuffs, with many refrigerated premises. On the north bank, in and near Queenhithe, furs may be landed at general wharves for the fur quarter of the City at Garlick Hill, just west of Cannon Street Station. On the south bank the pattern extends further upstream, as far as Waterloo Bridge opposite the eastern section of the Victoria Embankment. Here the general wharves are interrupted by several wharves dealing in newsprint and paper. Their warehouses act as convenient reservoirs of supply for the nearby machines in Fleet Street and the Southwark printing industry, south of London Bridge.

HAY'S WHARF

Downstream from London Bridge, the pattern of continuous general wharves is interrupted on the north bank of the Upper Pool by Billingsgate Market, the Custom House, and the Tower of London. Otherwise, general wharves predominate for two and three-quarter miles downstream from London Bridge on the north bank, and for two miles on the south bank. This probably reflects the difficulties of cross-river traffic to the more important hinterland of north London downstream from the London and Tower Bridges. Between these bridges on the south bank is the largest group of wharves under a single unified control to be found within *Pattern II*.

Three partners, who originally styled themselves the Proprietors of Hay's Wharf in 1862, by which name the business is still known, were an outstanding example of the combination of interests which are necessary to a successful wharf operation.[26] The initiator of the great enterprise, John Humphery, had rebuilt Hay's Wharf and developed a group of wharves west of London Bridge, all on the south side of the Upper Pool. He was a practical man of the river, well acquainted with the operation of the London lighterage trade. Unfortunately, this part of the riverside was severely damaged by a fire in 1861, and Alderman Humphery needed partners if he was to rebuild his organization to cope with the ocean-going vessels of the future. His choice of partners proved ideal.

Hugh Colin Smith came from a banking family with wide financial connections in the City of London. The third partner, Arthur Magniac, was a member of one of the oldest firms of merchant venturers, with interests in China and the Far East and with a fleet of tea clippers. At first, tea was the chief commodity handled. The combination of wharfinger, financier, and merchant proved very successful.

As early as 1867 the first consignment of New Zealand butter and cheese arrived, and, gradually, the firm expanded its ownership to wharves adjoining the original nucleus at Hay's. Today, with one exception, all the wharves on the south bank from Tower Bridge to London Bridge, with four upstream of this bridge, belong to Hay's Wharf.

Another important development of this firm was the consolidation of the provision trade on the south bank of the Upper Pool. Those concerned in this trade had previously concentrated their offices in Thames Street, behind the line of the old Legal Quays (see Figure 3). It became a policy of Hay's Wharf to develop Tooley Street (the name is a corruption of St. Olave's Street) as the main provision importing centre of the country. As the freeholds of premises in Tooley Street became vacant they were bought by the firm and leased to provision merchants. So successful has this policy been that practically all London provision merchants of note have their offices in Tooley Street. The London Provision Exchange, which serves the provision trade, has the magnificent and appropriate address of Number One London Bridge. More offices have recently been provided because this trade has increased since the war with the increase in the population of Greater London. Many of the new towns near London are fed through London's larder door of Tooley Street.

There are eight steamer berths for vessels up to the 3,000-ton (net) class, and one berth in Hay's Dock for vessels up to 600 tons. The limiting factor for ships is length; if they are longer than 420 feet, they are berthed with difficulty. Almost all the ships come from the continent of Europe, about twenty of them a week.

Vessels normally arrive on special days, like a regular train service. For example, at the lower berth of Cotton's Wharf, adjacent to Hay's Wharf upstream, a Danish vessel arrives every Monday and Wednesday, with a Dutch vessel in between times. Pigs slaughtered in Denmark towards the end of the week provide the cargo of vessels loading at Danish ports on Friday and Saturday. Ships will be voyaging across the North Sea on Sunday when ports are not working.

All Australian and New Zealand dairy produce is lightered from the Royal and Tilbury Docks by the associated lighterage firm of Messrs. Humphery and Grey (Lighterage) Ltd. in insulated barges with the distinctive trade mark of the Maltese Cross. Hay's Wharf has special contracts for Australian and New Zealand produce which is landed under the supervision of the respective national Dairy Produce Control Board. Long experience in the handling of these goods is vital to the meeting of the strict requirements laid down.

The electric cranes have slender jibs of a great height, able to carry two tons at an extreme radius of eighty feet. These features enable them to work the loopholes of a warehouse seven storeys high, and they can plumb the other side of a ship even if she has a beam of fifty feet.

The warehouses of Hay's Wharf have accommodation for about 104,000 tons of goods: 25,000 tons in cold stores; 9,000 tons in cool air stores; and 70,000 tons in general warehouses. The following table gives a summary of this group's accommodation. In the cool air stores are cheese (42–45°F.) and eggs (32°F.); in the cold stores are found bacon (14–16°F.), butter (12–14°F.), meat (10–12°F.), and green peas and other fresh vegetables (6°F.).

Five other interesting features of Hay's Wharf may be noted.

The wharves of this group upstream of London Bridge are served entirely by barges—a modern version of the restriction to navigation caused by the furthest downstream fixed bridge. City workers, who watch this part of the port during their lunch hour, all crowd against the downstream parapet of London Bridge; it is much more interesting to see the discharge of ships rather than that of barges. Internal movement of goods between the various wharves of the Hay's Wharf group can be accomplished either

TABLE XVIII

*Features and Accommodation of the Hay's Wharf Group*
*(South Bank of the Upper Pool)*

West to East

| Name of Wharf | Special Features | Covered Accommodation Thousands cu. ft. |
|---|---|---|
| Pickford's ... ... | — | 400 |
| St. Mary Overy's ... | — | 380 |
| New Hibernia ... ... | Cold and cool stores ⎫ | |
| Old Hibernia ... ... | — ⎬ | 3,000 |

Here is LONDON BRIDGE

| | | |
|---|---|---|
| Fenning's ... ... | — ⎫ | |
| Sun ... ... ... | — ⎬ | 1,250 |
| Topping's ... ... | — ⎭ | |
| Hay's Wharf Head Office | | |
| Chamberlain's ... ... | Cool store ... ... ⎫ | |
| Cotton's ... ... | Cold store ... ⎬ | 7,500 |
| Hay's ... ... ... | — ⎭ | |
| Willson's ... ... | Wine and Spirits storage ... ... | 3,000 |
| ,, ... ... | Cold store ... ... | — |
| Symon's ... ... | Cool store ... ... | 2,500 |
| St. Olave's ... ... | — | 300 |
| Mark Brown's ... | Cold store ... ... | 5,500 |
| ,, | Cool store to be completed in 1957 | |
| ,, | Jetty parallel to wharf | |

Here is TOWER BRIDGE

23,830

by water (barge) or by road. It is an interesting practical commentary on the contrast between water and road transport to find that the former would be used if the consignment weighed more than five tons in bulk.

The head office was built in 1931 on stilts, to allow parking space and easier access to the quays.

Chamberlain's and Cotton's Wharves may be compared. The former is an old warehouse, eight storeys high, with the loopholes serving as entrances to each floor directly above one another. A modern design, as in the adjacent Cotton's Warehouse, ensures that the loopholes are staggered so that a crane working one floor does not block others.

Mark Brown's Wharf is equipped with a jetty which has accommodation for two ships, each 420 feet long. Barges can lie between the jetty and the warehouse, a lay-out very reminiscent of the dolphins on the south side of King George V Dock.

Wines and spirits are stored in the cellars of Willson's Wharf. An extension across Tooley Street occurred in the 1920s when rum began to be stored in thirty arches beneath London Bridge Station. After the rum has matured in casks for three years, Hay's Wharf undertakes the bottling and labelling for a famous brand. Coffee is also bulked, sized and cleaned, when required. It is interesting to compare these developments from the simple port and warehouse function with the similar developments at the London and St. Katharine Dock system.

RIVERSIDE WHARVES DOWNSTREAM OF LONDON BRIDGE

Though it may appear invidious to single out further individual wharfinger companies from such a large and important group as *Pattern II*, the installations of three more firms may be briefly mentioned.

Messrs. New Fresh Wharf Ltd. operate premises adjacent to London Bridge on the north bank downstream, on the site of three of the old Legal Quays. These are the closest steamer wharf and associated warehouses to the centre of the City of London. Ships up to 500 feet in length can be accommodated, and five $1\frac{1}{2}$-ton cranes serve a ten-storey warehouse. This company specializes in the handling of fresh fruit and vegetables, dried fruit, canned goods, and rubber, for which there are four million cubic feet of covered storage available. Bonded accommodation exists for all goods except wine, spirits, and tobacco.

Chambers Wharf and Cold Stores, one mile below London Bridge on the south bank close to Tower Bridge, have berthing accommodation for three vessels at any one time and each may be up to 200 feet long. Among the vessels dealt with are those equipped with cooling or deep freezing facilities, and also a regular service for general cargo which arrives three times a week from Amsterdam. The Company operating the wharves specializes in the handling of highly perishable goods. There are approximately three and a half million cubic feet of covered storage space, of which one and half million cubic feet consist of modern refrigerated accommodation. Three-quarters of this is at very low temperature for 'quick frozen' goods, this being the largest sub-zero storage in the country.

Metropolitan and New Crane Wharves are situated on the north bank of the river, due south of the Shadwell New Basin (London Docks), about one and a quarter miles below London Bridge. A range of thirty seven-, six-, and four-storey warehouses adds up to covered accommodation of 4,600,000 cubic feet on 254 floors. Ships up to 1,500 tons (net) may be berthed, and a bewildering variety of goods is dealt with at these wharves: coffee, cocoa, tea, rubber, gums, spices, metals, wines and spirits, tallows, fruit juices, and canned goods; and the company have recently installed tanks for the storage of vegetable oils.

All such wharves have to be served by a road parallel to the river.[27] Reference to the front endpaper will demonstrate these roads: St. Katharine's Way; High Street, Wapping; and Wapping Wall, on the north: and Rotherhithe Street on the south. Often the warehouses have expanded across these roads to premises which are connected by overhead ways and conveyors.

Behind the wharves of *Pattern III* the longitudinal street is further back from the river, as can clearly be seen around the Isle of Dogs on the front endpaper. This is an indication that wharves dealing with goods in bulk demanding wider storage space are more numerous than the general wharves. On a windy day passengers on the river soon notice the lack of protection from the low premises of *Pattern III*; the multi-storey general warehouses of wharves upstream are excellent wind-breaks.

Indeed, there are few general wharves below the entrance to the West India Docks, six miles below London Bridge. The diagram, Figure 7, reveals how sharp this boundary is on both banks of the river.

*Pattern IV* now begins. The 'bulk wharves' predominate, but there are many wharves catering for the needs of river traffic : ship and tug repairers, and barge builders and repairers, are common. In Woolwich Reach, eight to ten miles below London Bridge, *Pattern IV* has undergone a change, for bulk wharves serving industrial premises are almost continuous. These premises have already been mentioned at the end of the section on the Royal Docks (*q.v*).

Beyond the entrances to the Royal Docks, ten miles below London Bridge, a sharp boundary denotes another profound change in the riverfront. *Pattern V* is made up of widely spaced bulk wharves and wharves serving public utilities. There are wide intervals alternately on each side of the river, a state of affairs which continues to the eastern limits of London River. As this pattern covers nearly twenty miles of riverside, and much more if the Sea Reach oil refineries are included, a separate discussion is necessary. The riverside wharves which make up *Pattern V*, though indisputably carrying out a port function, are best regarded in the light of the industial development of Lower Thameside.

## REFERENCES

1. The opposition of the Legal Quay owners was overcome by purchase.

2. 'In order to be exempted, the lighter must be bona fide engaged in the operation of either discharging or receiving the goods, so that where she enters for the purpose of discharging her cargo into a vessel and the cargo is shut out, with the result that she leaves the dock still loaded, she cannot claim exemption. Neither can she claim exemption if she enters for the purpose of discharging her cargo into a vessel from which the cargo is shut out and she then discharges it into another vessel which was not in the dock at the time when the lighter entered it.' H. Le Mesurier, *The Law Relating to the Port of London Authority* (Butterworth, 1934), 61–2.

3. C. L. Wheble, *The London Lighterage Trade: Its History, Organization and Economics* (Unpublished thesis, M.Sc. (Econ.), University of London, 1939), 244. These figures have been reduced to the nearest ten because of the great difficulty of knowing with greater accuracy the numbers of craft in effective

commission at any one time. 'The expression "craft" means and includes any lighter or barge or other like craft for conveying goods or any tug propelled by steam or any other motive power either wholly or partly within the limits of the Port of London . . .', *Port of London (Consolidation) Act*, 1920, Section 197. The terms lighter and barge are now synonymous.

4. To prevent congestion in the docks, tonnage charges are levied in cases where barges enter a dock earlier than two tides before the arrival of a ship for which they are bound, or remain more than three tides after completing their work.

5. C. L. Wheble, *op. cit.*, 224-5.

6. *Ibid.*, 228-31.

7. Just as the present rates on vessels and the free entry for barges indirectly subsidize the lighterage trade.

8. L. R. Jones, *The Geography of London River* (Methuen, 1931), 44-6, 110-1.

9. *Colliery Year Book*, 1956, 506.

10. The boundaries of this division coincide with the Metropolitan Police District.

11. Foreign coal from French ports and from other West European countries, or from the U.S.A. and Canada transhipped at Rotterdam and Antwerp, is now expected to diminish in quantity. From 1951-5 inclusive London's share of the national total of imported coal was 44%. *Annual Statement of the Trade of the United Kingdom, Vol. IV Supplement, 1951 and 1954.* (H.M. Customs and Excise, H.M.S.O., 1953 and 1956.) The 1955 total has been supplied by H.M. Customs and Excise, Bill of Entry Section, Statistical Office.

12. The following are, or will be, partially oil-fired power stations: Bankside, A and B; Barking C; Tilbury; and Belvedere (near Erith).

13. E. M. Rawstron, 'The Salient Geographical Features of Electricity Production in Great Britain', *Advancement of Science*, VII (1955), 73-82.

14. 'The expression "wharfinger" means the occupier of a wharf quay warehouse or granary adjoining the Port of London mainly used for warehousing the goods imported into the Port of London of persons other than the occupier of such premises.' *Port of London Act*, 1908, Section 49.

15. A. Smith, *The Wealth of Nations* (1776 edition), II, 424.

16. G. R. Stocks, 'Free Trade Zones and Re-Export Reliefs', *The Dock and Harbour Authority*, 27 (1946), 137–8; and R. S. Thoman, 'Foreign Trade Zones of the United States', *Geographical Review*, XLII (1952), 631–45.

17. 'The reasons for entrusting it [the future P.L.A.] with the control of the River and of the Docks do not apply with the same force to the case of the Warehouses [indicating those of the riverside wharves]. The requirements of the Port in this respect appear to have been sufficiently met by private capital and enterprise.' *Report of the Royal Commission on the Port of London* (Cd. 1151, H.M.S.O., 1902).

18. H. Atton and H. H. Holland, *The King's Customs* (Murray, 1910), II, 22.

19. The West India Docks had legal quays and bonded warehouses for cotton, mahogany, molasses, pimento, and rum from the West Indies; and cocoa, sugar, and coffee from any place. In the London Docks there were similar privileges for rice, tobacco, and wines and spirits other than from the West Indies.

20. *History of the Port of London*, II, 413.

21. In this section 'wharves' include jetties.

22. Based on Thameside and River and Canal Surveys, 1950. Unpublished material held by the Architect to the London County Council. *See* also *Administrative County of London Development Plan 1951: Analysis* (London County Council, 1951), 81–92. On August 10, 1956, the British Transport Commission Waterways Division announced that it would devote nearly 16% of its £5½ million national expenditure on modernization to the River Lea between Enfield Lock and the Thames. Larger and faster craft will use the river which in 1955 transported two million tons of goods, half of which was coal for north-east London power stations.

23. 'It will be appreciated that these figures refer only to the total number of separate wharves, and so give no indication of their relative significance or the importance of the undertakings by whom they are provided.' *Report by Docks and Inland Waterways Executive on Review of Trade Harbours 1948–50* (1951), 37.

24. In analysing the patterns shown in Figure 7, the following reservations must be borne in mind. The schematic representation of

the river irons out the curves of the river meanders so that the relative spacing of the properties is not accurate; they are too close together on the concave bank of the meander and too far apart on the convex bank. Wharves serving refrigerated premises were classed as general wharves; wharves operated by British Railways were classed as wharves dealing with goods in bulk. Exports were not considered; the only wharves dealing exclusively with exports are those owned by local authorities for the removal of refuse by barge. Finally, the diagram represents wharves with the same function by the same symbol irrespective of their greatly varying sizes and capacities.

25. This pattern of bulk wharves is extended along the lower Lea (within the County of London), the eastern two miles of the Grand Union (Regent's Canal), and Limehouse Cut (*see* front endpaper).

26. The history of the firm may be found in A. Ellis, *Three Hundred Years on London River: the Hay's Wharf Story, 1651–1951* (Bodley Head, 1952). Below, in the text, the correct name, The Proprietors of Hay's Wharf Ltd., is shortened to Hay's Wharf for convenience.

27. This of course does not apply to the six steamer quays of the Regent's Canal Dock (which deal with general cargo, including fruit), now administered by British Transport Waterways (*see* front endpaper).

# CHAPTER VII

# THE INDUSTRIAL DEVELOPMENT OF LOWER THAMESIDE[1]

DURING the present century there has been notable industrial development on the Lower Thameside marshes downstream from the main entrance to the Royal Docks. Isolation had previously been the chief characteristic of these marshes. Riparian settlements at Woolwich, Erith, and Gravesend were founded entirely on chalk bluffs. The original isolation explains the siting on the marshes of sewage farms, explosives works, the Royal Arsenal at Woolwich, W.D. property, and isolation hospitals. Arable farming is restricted to the inner margins because of the water-logged subsoil. Thus, except where small areas have been par-celled out for allotments and works' playing-fields, the marshes back from the river are mostly unimproved; the industries are almost exclusively concerned with the facilities afforded by river-front sites.

INDUSTRIES

Figure 8 is a location diagram and shows that the industries of Lower Thameside may be classified into five types. The geographical background of these industries will first be examined under these group headings, and then the general phenomenon of Thameside industrial development will be discussed.

*Public Utilities*

There are seventeen electricity power stations on the Thames, of which four occur on Lower Thameside, including the largest at Barking. Of the six gas works on the Thames, only the largest at Beckton is situated on Lower Thameside. Beckton Gas Works and Barking Electricity Generating Station are close together on the north side of the river, on opposite sides of Barking Creek (River Roding). Both these establishments are among the largest of their kind in Europe. Beckton carbonizes an average of 4,800 tons of coal every day; Barking may consume as much as 7,000 tons on a winter day. With such enormous fuel requirements it it vitally necessary that coal should be imported in bulk by water. There are other reasons for riverside location. Such installations require huge acreages for their site; they should be to leeward of large areas of settlement and isolated for aesthetic reasons. In addition, generating stations need huge amounts of water, 600 tons for every ton of coal burnt, in order to condense the steam after it has done its work in turning the turbine, and the Thames is the supplier.[2]

*Cement Works*

Cement production is a complicated technical process, and since it uses very bulky raw materials it must be sited near them. A situation on Thameside not only conforms to this rule but also provides additional advantages of tide-water communication. Although the raw materials vary somewhat and therefore affect the proportions used, the manufacture of 100 tons of cement requires a total of about 200 tons of chalk and clay combined, the proportion of clay varying from 25 to 30%. In addition to this about 30 to 35 tons of coal are used.

Proximity to chalk and clay and to water communication for fuel imports are therefore prime considerations. On Thameside sea-borne coal undercuts rail-hauled Kent coal. London Clay overlies the Chalk near Purfleet, and south of the river the Swanscombe outlier fortuitously brings clay close to workings in the Chalk, though at present most of the Swanscombe works receive alluvial clay via river barges from a pit near Cliffe. At Cliffe there is also an anticlinal ridge of the Chalk (*see* Figure 1) which is quarried for cement. This ridge can be traced westwards and reappears as the Purfleet anticline. This inlier of the Chalk, originally about one hundred feet high, has been breached in many places by gigantic pits, dug down to river level. On the south bank of the river at Erith, Northfleet, and Gravesend, cement works quarry the bluffs which the river has carved out of the Chalk dip-slope. Excavations have taken place on a huge scale, for chalk had been quarried here for centuries before the cement

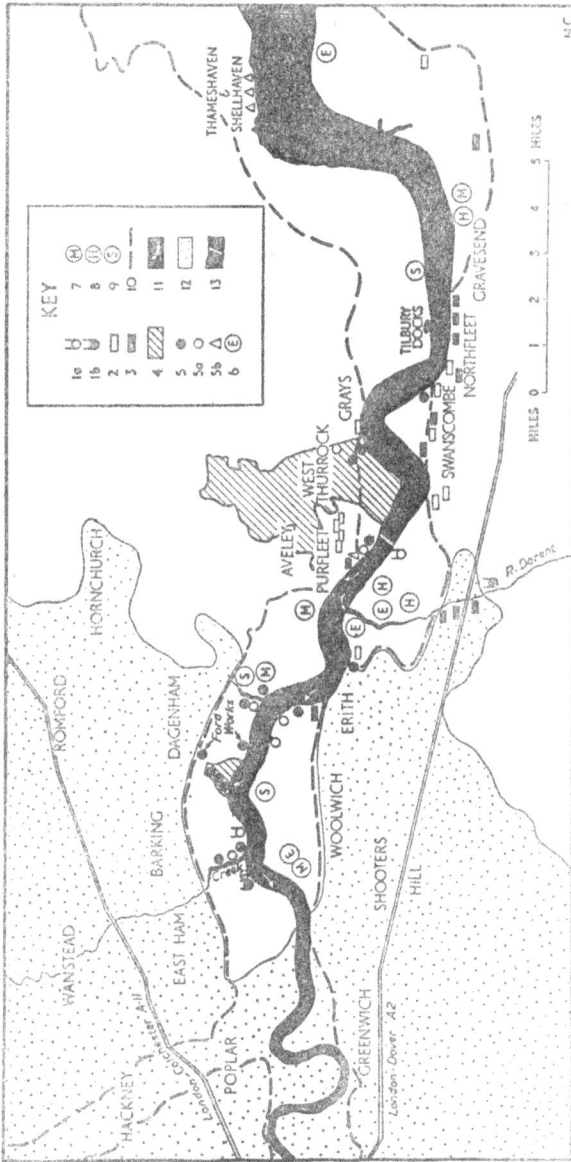

FIG. 8.—Industries of Lower Thameside.

1. Public Utilities (1a. Electricity Generating Stations; 1b. Gas Works). 2. Cement Works. 3. Paper Mills. 4. Industrial Estates. 5. Consumers' Goods Industries (5a. Timber Storage and Processing; 5b. Oil Storage and Processing). 6. Explosives Works. 7. Military Establishments. 8. Hospitals. 9. Sewage Works. 10. Inner Boundary of Thames and Lea Marshes. 11. Major Coal Landing Points, other than 1–5 above. 12. Continuously Built-up Area of London. 13. Dartford-Purfleet Tunnel.

Reproduced, by kind permission, from *Geography*.

K

industry accelerated the process after 1890. The quarries extend as far south as the London-Dover A2 road, and many houses and roads are left perched on artificial spines of land, creating planning problems in an area of competing land use.[3] It seems most common for cement works to be sited on the floor of old quarries. This makes rail communication with Thameside jetties easier for then there is little gradient, and chalk and clay may be gravity fed to the kilns. Thameside cement works account for half the production of Great Britain.

*Paper Mills*

Like the cement works, the paper mills depend on water communication. The manufacture of 100 tons of medium quality printing paper requires approximately 150 tons of mechanical pulp, 17 tons of dry sulphite pulp, 10 tons of china clay, and 70 tons of coal. Obviously, tide-water sites are an advantage for the importation of such large quantities of raw material in bulk. Two other factors have favoured Lower Thameside: Dartford has had an historical association with the paper industry from the time when an early mill was established there in 1588; and, of course, London is the nation's largest market for paper of all varieties, but particularly for newsprint and for fibre boards which are used extensively in packaging goods. Thus while the paper industry is sited physically adjacent to the cement industry, it manifests a contrast economically. The cement industry is situated on Thameside because of tide-water communication for fuel and the proximity of chalk, the principal raw material; the paper industry is situated on Thameside because of tide-water communication for fuel *and* raw materials and the proximity of London, its principal market.

The two largest mills in the country producing newsprint are to be found near Northfleet, and newsprint is the most important type of paper in volume manufactured in this part of Kent. Most mills produce a wide variety of paper goods, given an easy import of wood, pulp, and esparto grass, which can be combined with domestic supplies of waste paper, pulp wood, and rags. A modern paper mill can produce any desired quality of paper by the various mechanical and chemical methods of paper-making.

*Industrial Estates*

A relatively new method of fostering industrial development is the 'industrial estate'. Such an estate on Lower Thameside comprises a stretch of riverfront and adjacent land made ready for industry. This entails land consolidation and drainage, wharf and road building, and the provision of improved sites for lease by industrial concerns. In the marshland a great deal of capital has to be expended to be recouped slowly by rental charges. Even large industrial concerns cannot afford the huge double capital outlay required for first reclaiming and preparing the site, and then building the factory upon it.

The land on which the Ford Motor Company's factory is sited was originally made available by the industrial estate at Dagenham Dock, sited very near the old Dagenham Breach. The land was purchased by the industrial estate company in 1886, and by 1894 thirty acres of marsh had been built up to a height of twelve feet and level with the top of the old river wall. Most of the spoil used consisted of material excavated in the construction of London's underground railways. The concerns on this estate work up or store imported materials and despatch the products for the home market, so that exported cargoes only total 50% of those landed. At the West Thurrock Estate development is on similar lines, but in a more youthful stage. The most notable arrival there so far is a modern giant soap factory; there is a building joinery works, using imported timber, a dairy equipment factory, and many smaller plants. Part of the estate hinterland is leased as several chalk quarries for cement, and for sand and ballast excavations; eighty-six acres of riverside land have been purchased for a projected power station. At three jetties on the Thames the estate operates as a wharfinger. The Dartford-Purfleet Tunnel is being constructed immediately to the west, so that the situation of the estate, as will be seen later, is favourable to its fuller industrial development.

*Consumers' Goods Industries*

The largest concern in this group is the Ford Motor Company Ltd. with its associated wheel and car body factories. As is often emphasized, the company is unique in southern England in possessing its own blast furnace and coke ovens, so that cars and tractors (1,500 units per day) are made here out of the raw iron.[4] This underlines the excellent coal and raw material transport to Thameside, and the early realization of this by the company is due to the success achieved on an analogous site by the parent firm on the river Rouge, near Detroit. The original far-sighted decision to build a Thameside factory was recalled by Henry Ford himself in these words:

'We picked out the Dagenham site because it has water, rail and motor transport, and we can therefore put into it everything that we have learned at the River Rouge about the economic handling of materials.'[5]

Sugar refining, oilseed crushing, and timber storage and processing, are extensions of activities formerly carried on exclusively upstream of the main entrance to the Royal Docks. One unusual timber installation deserves a special note. Frog Island, Rainham, is a north bank peninsula formed where Rainham Creek makes a slightly deflected entrance into the Thames, fifteen miles below London Bridge. The tidal range of twenty-two feet leaves the berths dry at low tide so that ships and barges could only come alongside Frog Island near high tide. However, in 1948 the Phoenix Timber Company Ltd., which has a large timber depot on the Rainham Marshes, bought up components of the Mulberry Harbour used at Arromanches for the D-Day invasion of Europe. Mulberry Pier is now a floating jetty 412 feet long, connected to the river bank at Frog Island by a floating bridge 180 feet long. Two ships can be accommodated always afloat, for there are twenty-two feet at L.W.S.T.

All the industries mentioned so far are served by wharves which make up *Pattern V*, recognized in the previous chapter. Beyond London River along the borders of Sea Reach, there is a further final Thameside pattern which is most conveniently included here under *Consumers' Goods Industries*.

The oil refineries of consumer countries illustrate the difference in the concepts of site and situation. The modern oil tanker fleet commonly includes vessels of the 20,000 gross tonnage class. It follows that the situation of the largest and most modern oil refineries must be close to tidal approaches of sufficient depth for such large vessels. Such first-class approaches are no doubt already serving some of our biggest ports. Despite modern safeguards, port authorities naturally prefer that the refinery should have an isolated site in order that other port installations should not be damaged in case of fire. So it comes about that our modern refineries have a situation on the approaches to a great port but are isolated in their site.

The oil installations alongside Sea Reach illustrate this principle. In 1872 the Thames Conservancy prohibited vessels laden with petroleum from proceeding westwards of Thameshaven, a limit which was confirmed in 1904 at the Mucking Light. This is the light at the western end of Sea Reach, and it was chosen because to the west the river narrows considerably (see the discussion in Chapter III, page 54), and it was thought that damage to shore installations would be thereby increased. Petroleum had to be transferred to special barges in order to travel up London River.

The decision was taken at a time when petroleum was handled in a primitive way, and when fears outran the risks involved. Despite much opposition, the Mucking Light remained until 1938 when a limit at Crayfordness, opposite Purfleet, came into force. By this time the nuclei of the oil installations were established alongside Sea Reach, and since 1938 the greatly increased size of vessels has precluded the use of upstream sites.[6]

The sites used at present are in two groups. The Shellhaven-Thameshaven group comprises the London and Thameshaven Oil Wharves Ltd., perhaps the world's largest 'public oil wharfingers', operating a depot here since 1876; the Shell installations; the refineries at Coryton,[7] east of Thameshaven, of Messrs. Cory Bros. —Vacuum Oil Company Ltd., with a new refinery completed in 1954; and the depot of the London and Coastal Oil Wharves Ltd., on the south-west tip of Canvey Island. The other group is not on the Kent shore opposite as one might expect because the water access is impeded by a continuous line of mudbanks and sands. Instead, the site is on the western peninsula formed by the confluence of the Medway and the Thames, the so-called Isle of Grain (see Figure 1). Here are the installations of the Anglo-Iranian Oil

Company Ltd., actually on the left bank of the river Medway where the deepest water is available.[8] These two groups form the largest oil-refining area in Europe, with almost a third of the total U.K. refining capacity.

TABLE XIX

*Thames-Medway Oil Refineries Average Annual Capacity*

(Thousands of metric tons)

|  | 1937[9] | 1955[10] |
|---|---|---|
| Shell Refining & Marketing Co., Ltd., Shellhaven | 800 | 3,700 |
| Anglo-Iranian Oil Co., Ltd., Isle of Grain ... | — | 4,600 |
| Vacuum Oil Co., Ltd., Coryton ...    ...    ... | 250 | 1,000 |
| Berry Wiggins & Co., Ltd., Kingsnorth ...   ... | 90 | 100 |
| London & Thameshaven Oil Wharves Ltd., Thameshaven    ...    ...    ...    ...    ... | 400 | — |
|  | 1,540 | 9,400 |
| Total U.K.    ...    ...    ...    ... | 4,210 | 29,675 |

The common element of all these industries is that they make use of heavy raw materials or fuel and thus derive considerable benefit from the water highway of the Thames. On the opposite side of London the Great West Road plays a somewhat similar role, but the factories it supplies house lighter industries. As is well known, water transport is most economic for heavy bulk cargoes undergoing long journeys, *i.e.* for raw materials and fuel. Road transport has much greater flexibility and is suitable for carrying small, irregular loads relatively short distances, *i.e.* for the distribution of finished products. This contrast is due to the fact that water carriers had high terminal charges and low running costs and operate as large transport units; road carriers have negligible terminal charges but relatively high running costs and must of necessity operate as small transport units.

This principle may be conveniently illustrated along the road leading to Barking Generating Station (Figure 9). When this road was built in 1925 it became apparent that flanking it was a series of excellent industrial sites. From the diagram it is seen that establishments on the west side of the road will have the advantage of water communication, originally cheap land, and good inland communications with the vast market and labour supply of London's eastern suburbs. Establishments on the east side of the road enjoy the same advantages with the exception of

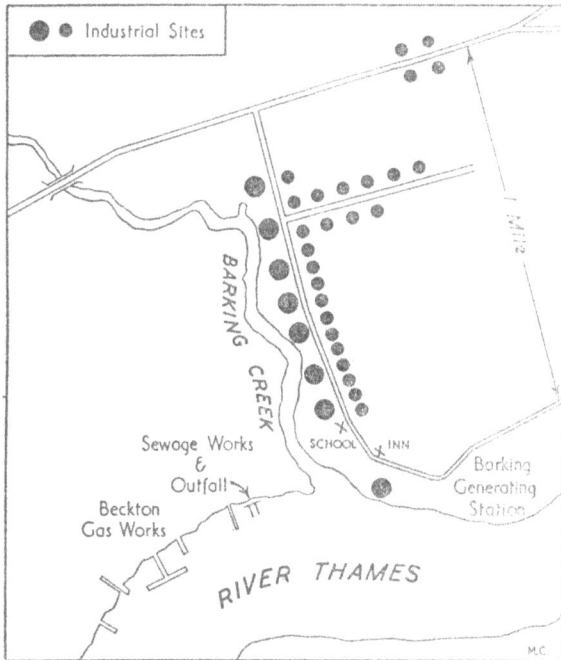

FIG. 9.—Industrial Establishments along River Road, Barking.
Reproduced, by kind permission, from *Geography*.

direct water communication. This exception, however, causes a great contrast in the types of industry to east and west. Typical of industries to the west are the production of concrete building materials, tin and wolfram, and zinc oxide; there are also timber and oil storage depots. To the east are found such industries as light engineering, synthetic rubber products, printing ink, and chemists' patent products. In addition there are seven under-takings on the west side of the road occupying approximately the same length of road frontage as fourteen on the east. This is to be expected, for a waterside site implies a requirement for the delivery of bulky raw materials, which in turn necessitates a large site for storage and processing. The opposite sides of River Road thus graphically stress the contrast between the large, sprawling riverside factory dominated by its raw material, and the roadside factory which is typically compact, often completely masking its activities by a neat if sometimes precious façade. Undoubtedly, the industries of Lower Thameside are of the former type.

### THE PATTERN OF DEVELOPMENT

Bearing this in mind, together with the analysis of industries by groups, the general pattern of Thameside industrial development may be examined by considering the example of a hypothetical port situated at an estuary head, punctuating the deductive argument by reference to observed fact. Figure 10 (a) shows such a theoretical port as it might have appeared in the early nineteenth century. The heavy industries would have stood close to the point where goods were landed, *i.e.* the port centre, because of the deficiencies then of transport by land. For the same reason the workers would have been close at hand, mainly within walking distance. Moreover, the city centre was the best place from which to distribute the finished products. However, as far as the import of raw materials was concerned any point along the estuary was as good as the city centre for unloading bulk goods which did not have to be re-sorted to many destinations; but certain requirements must be met before industry will come to the estuary shores. Transport inland must be efficient enough to overcome the comparative isolation of riverside sites. Engineering technique must be competent to deal with the unstable terrain and swampy conditions of an estuarine flood-plain. These two requirements have in fact been met only during the present century.

It may next be asked whether any economic principle limits industrial extension down the estuary shores. Figure 11 is a simple graph showing how costs of prime importance for any industry vary relatively to each other from the port centre seawards. As has been shown above, raw materials can be landed anywhere in

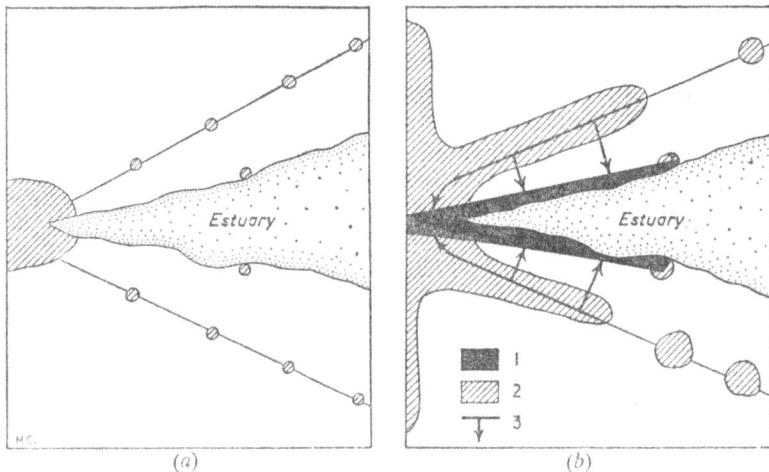

FIG. 10.—(a) A Hypothetical Port in the Early Nineteenth Century. (b) The Same Port Today. 1. Heavy industry. 2. Settlements. 3. Routes of daily migration by industrial workers.

Reproduced, by kind permission, from *Geography*.

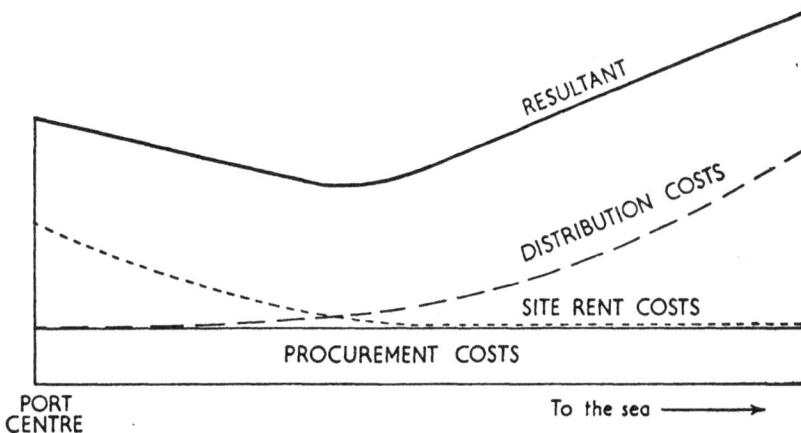

RESULTANT

DISTRIBUTION COSTS

SITE RENT COSTS

PROCUREMENT COSTS

PORT
CENTRE

To the sea ⟶

FIG. 11.—Factors in the Costs of Manufacture for Waterside Sites.

Reproduced, by kind permission, from *Geography*.

the estuary where there are berthing facilities without variation in cost. So procurement costs remain stable. Site rent costs and land values naturally decrease away from the port centre until a minimum is reached. However, distribution inland becomes progressively more difficult as the distance from the port centre increases, and distribution costs will rise. They do not rise so steeply at first as site rent costs decrease because after all the industry is moving nearer some markets, and the flexibility of road transport may even be assisted by being released from the congested port centre. The resultant of these three sets of costs shows a steady decrease downstream until a point is reached beyond which steep rises in costs are encountered. It must be emphasized that these costs apply only to sites with river frontage, and thus development will take the form of an 'industrial gallery forest', with dead-end rail and road routes linking the riparian industry to the main radial lines of communication. In the case of London and the Thames, the point, beyond which there are great increases in costs, for all industries except petroleum refining, is at present found at Tilbury-Gravesend, twenty-six miles downstream from the city centre. Future developments, notably the opening of the Dartford-Purfleet Tunnel, will cause this point to shift further east.[11]

At the moment it is uneconomic to engage in riverfront industrial activity east of Gravesend. This is due to the situation of the most easterly of the Lower Thames marshes. Firstly, there is no chalk immediately accessible, and better sites for cement works are provided by the Medway water-gap crossing the North Downs a little to the east. Secondly, there is no easy way of transporting goods across the half-mile-wide river; this restricts the hinterland of any prospective riverside factory. Thirdly, the area is more than twenty-six miles downstream from London Bridge, a rather long haul to the centre of a potential market. These three disadvantages outweigh for the present the apparent advantages of inviting flat land, no doubt cheap, which borders the river. The marshes east of Gravesend are thus just the same as when the prison hulks, mentioned by Dickens, were anchored in the river; apart from the rifle range and a few cattle grazing desultorily on the rank grasses, the mournful landscape remains unchanged as it was in the great novelist's day. In any case plenty of riverside space is available west of Tilbury-Gravesend. *Pattern V* is still in its development stage—a pioneer industrial area which has not yet evolved to its full mature strength. While physical and economic factors may now combine to favour industrial development as far east as Gravesend, this cannot in fact flourish unless industrial workers are within range.

Again transport improvements have acted as a causal factor. The effect has been graphically described as the 'explosion of cities' (*see* Figure 10 (*b*) ), when concomitantly with population increase, more and more people live further and further away from the city centre. They wish to live further out for two reasons. Living conditions near the city centre are often poor, because of overcrowding; secondly, rent and land values are generally much lower in the city's suburbs. At first, almost all the suburban workers migrated along the main lines of communication, because they had to travel back and forth each day to the industrial centre. In the case of London the two main lines of communication to the east are London-Colchester and London-Dover. Between them settlement has ever eschewed the marshes because of the liability to flood, unstable foundations for building, and unhealthy conditions. [12] Yet today road transport now carries many thousands of workers daily between riverside factories and these main lines of London's eastward expansion. Vast new quasi-satellite towns at Harold Hill (near Romford, estimated population 27,000) and Aveley (19,000)[13] swell this labour supply for Thamesides industry (compare Figures 8 and 10 (*b*) ). Planning of population movement and industrial development seems assured of success if it follows the long-established trends so well apparent.

Such an outgrowth of industry downstream appears as a recent systematic development of general cargo ports situated at estuary heads. Bayonne on the Adour exhibits a similar development on a much smaller scale; Bordeaux has its industrial suburb of Bassens downstream; Rotterdam has seen industry move seawards to Schiedam and Vlaardingen. However, while the general application of such a scheme seems eminently logical, it must be remembered that in any evolution of this kind Greater London is likely to show the first and more remarkable symptoms because it is among the largest of general cargo ports and possesses the greatest population.

## REFERENCES

1. This chapter is based substantially on an article by the author which appeared under this title in *Geography*, XXXVII (1952), 89–96. Grateful acknowledgement is due to the Editor of the Geographical Association for permission to re-publish the text and diagrams.

2. For an analysis of the factors concerned in the location of power stations see E. M. Rawstron, 'The Distribution and Location of Steam-Driven Power Stations in Great Britain', *Geography*, XXXVI (1951), 249–62; 'The Salient Geographical Features of Electricity Production in Great Britain', *Advancement of Science*, VII (1955), 73–82; and 'Changes in the Geography of Electricity Production', *Geography*, XL (1955), 92–7. For further details on London's power stations *see* C. D. Harris, 'Electricity Generation in London, England', *Geographical Review*, XXXI (1941), 127–34.

3. A. Coleman, 'Landscape and Planning in Relation to the Cement Industry of Thames-side', *Town Planning Review*, XXV (1954), 216–30.

4. From 1944–56 the blast furnace produced two million tons of pig-iron without relining, a record for the British steel industry.

5. H. Ford and S. Crowther, *Moving Forward* (1930), 257. The extract is reproduced by permission of Messrs. Doubleday & Company Inc., publishers.

6. A concise history of the Lower Thames and Medway petroleum industry, including the post-war building of large-scale refineries 1945–51, is given by B. E. Cracknell, 'The Lower Thames and Medway Petroleum Industry', *Geography*, XXXVII (1952), 79–88.

7. *Cf.* Cubitt Town, Silvertown, Beckton, on formerly uninhabited marsh of the flood-plain.

8. Two small outliers of these groups should be noted: the storage depot of the Anglo-American Oil Company Ltd., at Purfleet, and the small refinery of Berry Wiggins & Company Ltd., at Kingsnorth, three miles west of the Isle of Grain.

9. Figures derived from a table in the *Petroleum Times*, November 5, 1948.

10. As at December 31, 1955; figures supplied by the Petroleum

Information Bureau. The Isle of Grain refinery will have an annual average capacity of seven million metric tons by 1958; by the end of 1958 a new crude distillation unit will have doubled the capacity of the Shellhaven refinery.

11. The Minister of Transport announced on April 19, 1956, that work on the Dartford-Purfleet Tunnel was to start in a few weeks, nearly seventeen years after the pilot tunnel was completed. The project should be finished by about 1962.

12. Tilbury was a notable, and unfortunate, exception (*see* Chapter V, p. 114). Some post-war houses have recently been built on the inner parts of the flood-plain, near River Road, Barking (Figure 9).

13. On land purchased from the West Thurrock Industrial Estate in 1945.

# CHAPTER VIII

# MARKETS AND TRADE

THE industries described in the last chapter depend on the port. In its turn the port depends on certain markets to control the movements of some of the goods passing through it. The expansion of the port has been traced from the confinement of Legal Quays in the sixteenth century to the present time when upon the banks of every reach of the tidal Thames some port function is carried out. On the other hand, the commodity markets which control, ease, and augment the movement of many of the cargoes through the port have remained within the precincts of the City of London. This is not mere inertia. Markets have to be in central places to provide equal ease of access for all their customers. Centrality in this case is determined by the financial machinery of the City which must be physically close to assist the complicated marketing operations. Here is one of the basic reasons for the crowding of exchange and financial functions within the City's famous 'square mile'.

COMMODITY MARKETS

These markets are the link between London the international financial centre, and London the port. As far as discussion of the port is concerned, the markets make up a separate subject which is nevertheless parallel and linked.

Figure 12 is an attempt to show this parallel linkage. The markets control much of the port's activity from a distance. As the port deals with the movements of goods according to the wishes of their owners, so the commodity markets deal with the movements of ownership. It will be appreciated that each commodity will have its own marketing operations which differ in some way from the simplified scheme shown on this diagram.[1]

For convenience, the markets may be divided into the following types: those now owned by the City Corporation and

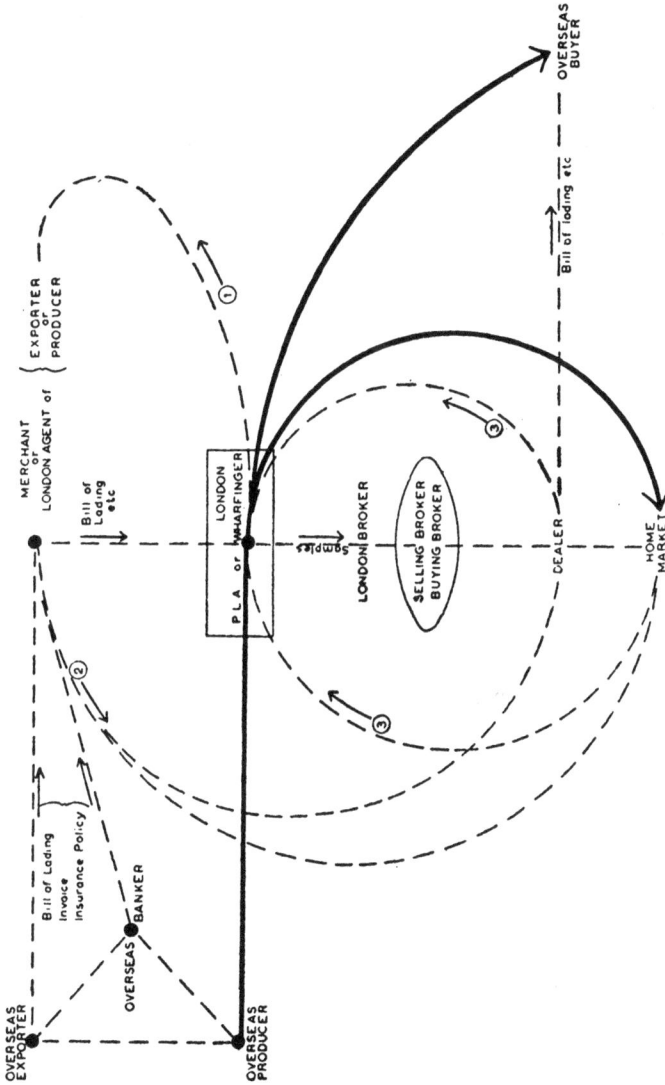

FIG. 12.—Port and Commodity Market: a Schematic Diagram to show their Interrelated Functions.

The physical movement of goods is represented by the continuous lines; communications by telegraph, telephone, and air and surface mail are shown by broken lines. The numbered arrows show the three main sequential movements of the dock or warehouse warrant. In the diagram the port function is contained within the small rectangle; the function of the commodity market within the ellipse beneath.

others, in which goods enter the market; other commodity markets where goods do not enter the market; markets dealing in 'futures'; and other markets where there is no set or formal meeting place for buyer and seller.

Markets owned by the City Corporation include Smithfield, Spitalfields, Leadenhall, and Billingsgate. None of Billingsgate's fish now passes through the port; it is brought by rail and road from ports nearer the fishing grounds. These markets, like those at Covent Garden, Borough, and Brentford, deal with domestic produce as well as imported food. For these reasons they are best considered later indirectly under the sections dealing with imported meat and fruit.

The remaining markets are the rooms where brokers meet who represent the merchants and dealers in the various trades. If the commodity to be sold varies with each lot, it is necessary to sell by sample at an auction. Such are the characteristics of the wool, tea, and fur trades. Visits to the wool in the warehouses, inspection of samples in fur brokers' offices, and the ritual of tea tasting are necessary.

Other commodities may be easily standardized by written specification. Trading becomes more formal, and samples are scarcely necessary. Sale is made by transfer of the document of title, perhaps a dock or warehouse warrant. It is possible to go one step further and buy and sell standard descriptions of goods at a future date, sometimes up to eighteen months ahead.[2] Such 'futures' markets in London are in rubber, cocoa, shellac, sugar, and wool tops;[3] the four leading base metals, *i.e.* copper, tin, lead, and zinc;[4] and maize and barley.

A main role of the futures markets in these commodities is to allow traders to protect themselves against fluctuations in price by the practice known as hedging. Bizarre as it may seem, only a very small minority of futures contracts are allowed to terminate in the delivery of the commodities to which they refer; they are usually liquidated by making another contract which balances the original. Apart from the service to buyers and sellers, the operation of a futures market certainly helps to regulate the flow of the actual commodities through the port. The majority of the transactions dealing with these actual commodities takes place in the actuals markets.

Figure 13 shows that all these markets are to be found well within half a mile from the Bank of England in the eastern part of the City of London. Just as they derive benefit from being close to banks, clearing houses, insurance offices, and other linked markets, so in turn their members, brokers, and merchants in that trade find it an advantage to be close to them. Buying and selling of other commodities may take place in the City but in no

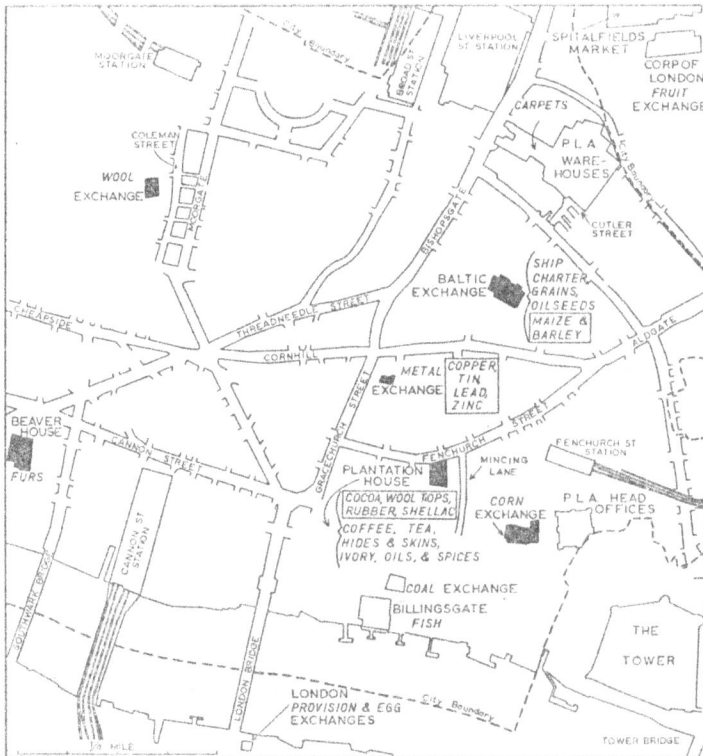

FIG. 13.—London Commodity Markets.

Markets which are held in private rooms under the auspices of the respective trade associations are shown in black. The names of commodities which appear inside a rectangle are those for which a 'futures' market exists. At the end of 1956 a further futures market was opened at Plantation House for sugar.

L

set or formal meeting place. Business may be done by telephone or in the offices of members of the trade.

At one time Mincing[5] Lane was the centre for the sale of many commodities because it was natural for merchants to have their premises along a highway from the City centre towards the Pool. Similarly, sales were made in a street parallel on the east, Mark (formerly Mart) Lane. In 1811, when a centre was required to succeed the various coffee-house rendezvous, a site in Mincing Lane was chosen. Unfortunately, the London Commodity Sale Rooms were destroyed by enemy action in 1941. In 1945 when marketing re-opened in London it was found convenient for the London Commodity Exchange to be set up in Plantation House,[6] only a hundred yards from the former Sale Rooms in Mincing Lane. This accounts for the wide variety of goods bought and sold within one building, with marketing under the control of the London Commodity Exchange Co., Ltd., since 1954.

The chartering of ships and aircraft and of space in them is carried on at the Baltic[7] Exchange because, as the full name of 'The Baltic and Mercantile Shipping Exchange' implies, there was an amalgamation of the original Baltic Exchange with the London Shipping Exchange in 1900. Both these exchanges had grown from seventeenth century coffee-houses. Much of the world's tramp steamer tonnage may be chartered here. Aircraft charter is also carried out. These are functions which transcend in scope the single Port of London.

Further details of some of these markets may be conveniently dealt with under the commodity in question in the following section.

GENERAL TRADE STATISTICS

The amount of information available is very great, and for more details the reader is directed to the sources on which this section has been based.[8]

The number of ships, foreign and coastwise, arriving and departing from the port is a little over 1,000 a week (since 1953), with a total net registered tonnage of 70,748,090 in the year ended March 31, 1956. This exceeded the record of the year ended March 31, 1954 which in turn had surpassed that of the previous year and the pre-war peak of 1937. Two main reasons can be adduced for this record traffic. The population of London and neighbouring towns which is supplied and fed through the port has increased in numbers since 1937. Secondly, the change in the type of the nation's export trade since the Second World War, with its increased emphasis on the export of manufactured goods, has thrown a burden on the country's principal general cargo ports.

Of the total net registered tonnage using the port just under half entered the docks of the P.L.A. during 1947–56, or just under a third of the number of ships. During the same decade a third of the net registered tonnage using the port was engaged in the coastwise trade. The total net registered tonnage of shipping using the port represented 18·5% of the total shipping using United Kingdom ports in the year ended March 31, 1954; and London dealt with 34·5% of the value of all merchandise imported into and exported from the country during the same year.

The following table shows more details of the port's trade during 1953–4:

TABLE XX

*Tonnages of London's Imports and Exports 1953–4*

Year ended March 31, 1954

(The total of 51,405,555 tons includes transhipments)

Where handled:

| | | |
|---|---|---|
| River ... ... ... ... ... ... | | 66·6% |
| Docks: | | |
|     by P.L.A. over quays ... ... | 8·2% | |
|     by tenants of the P.L.A. over | | |
|       quays ... ... ... ... | 5·6% | 33·4% |
|     transferred into barges ... ... | 19·6% | |

Imports, exports, and transhipments[9] in the year ended March 31, 1938 accounted for the following percentages of the total trade of the port, by weight: 78, 13·5, and 8·5; in the year ended March 31, 1954 the corresponding percentages were: 75·5, 17·5, and 7.

When *values* of foreign trade are analysed, imports do not

loom so large because of the much higher value of export goods and the fact that coastwise imports (notably coal) are not included in the tables of H.M. Customs. Imports, exports, and exports of imported merchandize in the calendar year 1938 accounted for the following percentages of the total trade of the port, by value: 69, 24, and 7; in the calendar year 1954 the corresponding percentages were: 56·5, 41, and 2·5.

Comparing the year ended March 31, 1954 with the year ended March 31, 1937 one finds that the amount of exports had risen by over three million tons. In 1953–4 the movement of imported goods over the dock quays represented only 12% of the total imports; but the dock quays handled 26·5% of the exported goods.

Statistics can be indigestible. Let the above facts be put more simply and inaccurately. London sees 1,000 arrivals and departures of ships each week, a fifth of the shipping using U.K. ports, carrying a third of the value of the country's imports and exports; these amount to fifty million tons of goods, of which one-seventh is handled over the dock quays, and imports account for three-quarters of the port's trade, by weight, but only a little over half by value (1954).

Some details of the imports and exports can now be considered. The procedure adopted below was as follows. Firstly, only commodities which had an imported or exported value of over £10 million in 1948 were considered.[10] This year was chosen because the port had by then recovered from the war, and the recent inflationary rise in prices had scarcely begun. It will be appreciated that much depends on the type of commodity classification made as to whether or not different types of cargo reach the arbitrarily chosen value of £10 million. The classification followed is based on that of H.M. Customs import and export lists.

IMPORTS

The chief imported commodities will now be discussed in *decreasing order of value* in London's trade of 1954 as in Table XXI. The expressions 'London's share (w)' and 'London's share (v)' refer to London's share of the weight or value of that commodity

TABLE XXI

*Imports into London,*[11] *1954 (worth over £10 million, 1948)*

| Imported Commodity | Value £ million 1954 | Percentage of Total U.K. Imports, by Value 1954 |
|---|---|---|
| Tea ... ... ... ... ... | 106·5 | 84 |
| Crude Petroleum ... ... ... ... | 63·9 | 29 |
| Raw Sheep's and Lambs' Wool ... | 54·8 | 30 |
| Unrefined Sugar ... ... ... ... | 53·8 | 58 |
| Timber ... ... ... ... ... | 49·2 | 32 |
| Butter ... ... ... ... ... | 40·7 | 42 |
| Metals (excluding Copper) and Manufactures thereof ... ... ... | 34·3 | 30 |
| Chilled and Frozen Mutton and Lamb... | 33·2 | 63 |
| Bacon (excluding Canned) ... ... | 31·8 | 45 |
| Chilled and Frozen Beef ... ... | 29·9 | 80 |
| Refined Petroleum ... ... ... | 27·9 | 32 |
| Paper-making Materials ... ... | 27·4 | 32 |
| Copper (Unwrought) ... ... ... | 26·2 | 27 |
| Paper, Paperboard, and Manufactures thereof ... ... ... ... ... | 24·8 | 48 |
| Machinery and Parts thereof (other than Electric) ... ... ... ... | 22·7 | 30 |
| Wheat ... ... ... ... ... | 21·6 | 24 |
| Fresh Fruit ... ... ... ... | 19·9 | 30 |
| Raw Rubber ... ... ... ... | 18·1 | 38 |
| Cereals (other than Wheat) and Cereal Preparations ... ... ... ... | 16·8 | 20 |
| Cheese ... ... ... ... ... | 16·7 | 61 |
| Hides and Skins (Undressed) ... | 14·1 | 32 |
| Tobacco ... ... ... ... ... | 13·8 | 18 |
| Vegetable Oils (Unrefined) ... ... | 13·3 | 38 |
| Wines and Spirits ... ... ... | 8·5 | 48 |
| Total of Imports ... ... | 1,167·0 | |

in the national trade. The post-war statistics in this analysis refer to the calendar years 1946 to 1954 inclusive; the pre-war calendar years considered for comparison were from 1934 to 1938 inclusive.[12] The figures in brackets after the italicised title of each commodity refer to the value, in £ million in 1954, of that commodity imported into London and also into other ports of the United Kingdom which have a major share of the trade.

Rather than present a great number of graphs and tables, the digestion of this mass of statistics is attempted largely by means of percentages and certain key words:

> Very slight refers to a change of less than 2%
> Slight refers to a change of       2– 5%
> Moderate refers to a change of   5–10%
> Notable refers to a change of    10–15%
> Great refers to a change of       15–20%
> Very great refers to a change of over 20%

*Tea* (London, 106·5 ; Liverpool, 10·0). Despite the high proportion of the nation's tea which comes to London, 80–85% in the period 1952 to 1954, this share (w and v) showed a moderate decrease on the port's pre-war share, probably due to the rise in importance of overseas auction centres. The average total amount imported into the country was almost the same as pre-war, but there was a fourfold increase in price.

Tea chests are generally discharged at Tilbury or the Royal Docks and taken by barge to 'up-town' warehouses to be drawn on by tea blenders after the auctions. A third of the tea sold at the world's auctions has been sold at Plantation House in post-war years.[13] The Tea Sample Distribution Centre is located in the Cutler Street Warehouses where samples from twenty-four London warehouses are collected at a central place for the convenience of merchants and brokers.

*Crude Petroleum* (London, 63·9 ; Southampton, 50·7 ; Manchester, 42·3). The phenomenal rise in imports of crude petroleum is a result of the post-war construction of giant refineries alongside Sea Reach (*see* pages 148–50). The following figures illustrate the enormous post-war increase (in million gallons): 1938, 82; 1947, 71 ; and 1954, 2,088.

*Raw Sheeps' and Lambs' Wool* (Hull, 55·9 ; London, 54·8 ; Liverpool, 40·8). London's post-war share (v) of this commodity showed a notable decrease over the pre-war share (v) ; between a quarter and a third of the country's total imports now enter the port.

London is no longer the world market for wool. Since the peak year of 1895, when 1·6 million bales were sold, the primary markets of producing countries have provided increasing competition. Improved shipping services between the wool-producing countries and France, Italy, Japan, etc., have been a contributory cause of the decline in London's wool turnover during this century. There was a drop in the London sales after both the First and Second World Wars, during which the auctions had been discontinued. At such times buyers were perforce brought into contact with other outlets. The primary markets also increased in importance during times of peace. Australian sheep farms have been gradually subdivided, and only the larger clips justify the grower who consigns his wool for sale on the London market. Before the Second World War the growth of the Japanese textile industry increased the importance of the Australian auctions because there was a considerable saving in freight rates on the Australia-Japan route when London was by-passed. After the Second World War similar considerations have applied to wool consigned to the U.S.A., which has recently emerged as a major wool importer.

The advantage of the London market is its excellent situation for the supply of 'spot' needs of the textile industries of western Europe. If a manufacturer finds that his overseas purchase falls short of his requirements, he can make up the deficiency of grade or quantity in London. The present (1953–5) average sale in London is 295,000 bales per annum in eight sales of two to four weeks' duration each. The main area of wool storage and display is in the Crescent Warehouse at London Dock and in neighbouring warehouses.

*Unrefined Sugar* (London, 53·8 ; Liverpool, 27·6). Imports of sugar, by weight, in the post-war period were slightly greater than pre-war, and London's share (v) of this increased trade was also slightly greater than pre-war. Transport of sugar in bulk has been a successful post-war development. Only half the labour at the loading port is needed ; discharge is at the rate of 2,000–4,000 tons per day, compared with 700–1,000 tons per day when the sugar is in bags. A 9,000-ton cargo of a new bulk sugar ship would cost £11,000 to put into bags (which have some residual value). Bulk transport of sugar will certainly become predominant.

Besides facilities in the South West India Dock, a large plant for handling raw sugar in bulk from vessels of 5,000 tons has been built at the Plaistow Wharf Refinery of Messrs. Tate and Lyle Ltd., Silvertown. One of the silos of this plant can store 40,000 tons of sugar.

Sugar refining developed near the ports traditionally dealing with imported sugar. According to Wilfred Smith's industrial classification,[14] it shares the highest degree of immobility with seed crushing and grain milling because of the bulkiness of the raw material. Concentration of sugar refining close to major importing ports is to be expected.

*Timber* (London, 49·2; Liverpool, 19·9). London's share (v) in the post-war period was very slightly below that of pre-war, which was a third of the nation's timber imports by value. Sawn timber now predominates. Hewn soft- and hardwoods accounted for only £5·3 million of the 1954 total, when the ratio of softwoods to hardwoods was three to one by value, or about three and a half to one by volume. The seasonal flush in the arrival of softwoods from the Baltic is now alleviated by regular imports from British Columbia.

*Butter* (London, 40·7; Liverpool, 12·6). The tonnage of the national imports of butter from 1952 to 1954 was about 60% of pre-war imports, and London's share (v) had declined slightly. A similar decrease is to be noticed in London's share (v) of cheese, possibly due to the loss of refrigerated accommodation in the war, especially near the Greenland and South Docks of the Surrey Commercial Dock system.

*Metals* (*excluding Copper*) *and Manufactures thereof* (London, 34·3; Liverpool, 15·3; Manchester, 10·9). Owing to the very miscellaneous nature of this group, comparison of London's 1954 share (v) with the pre-war trade does not seem useful. Iron and steel in one form or another accounted for £14·1 million of the 1954 total; lead £8·6 million; and zinc, £5·9 million. The imported 'manufactures of metals' amounted to only £4·1 million.

*Chilled and Frozen Mutton and Lamb* (London, 33·2; Liverpool, 11·3). London's share (w and v) still showed in 1954 a moderate decrease compared with its pre-war share, but bulk buying of meat had dominated the trade up to that time. About three and a half times more lamb than mutton comes to London and accounted for £29·4 million of the 1954 total. Frozen meat (10–15°F.)

arrives in hard condition and has to be thawed out before use; chilled meat (28–30°F.) is soft and ready for immediate consumption. The latter is more difficult to transport because the carcasses are stowed separately and need more careful handling at the ports. Besides cold stores adjacent to the Royal Docks, the P.L.A. maintains other stores in St. John Street (built in 1896) and Charterhouse Street (1914), close to West Smithfield, in order that the market shall have a stock of meat which can be drawn upon easily and quickly.

*Bacon (excluding Canned)* (London, 31·8; Liverpool, 2·5). London's share (w and v) from 1950 to 1954 showed a notable increase over its pre-war share of this commodity. The trade to London is now back to the pre-war average of about 130,000 tons annually.

*Chilled and Frozen Beef* (London 29·9; Liverpool, 8·4). By 1953 London regained its pre-war share (w and v), with a moderate increase in 1954, but the annual imports were running at about half the quantity of pre-war years. Chilled beef was not imported into this country after the war in any appreciable quantity until 1953; in the period immediately following, it soon increased to predominate over frozen beef in about the ratio of three to one.

*Refined Petroleum* (London, 27·9). London's post-war share (w and v) of this trade was slightly below pre-war, annual quantities being about five-eighths of the totals imported in pre-war years. The trade is now far surpassed by crude petroleum imports.

*Paper-making Materials* (London, 27·4). London's share (v) in post-war years was slightly below pre-war, but it still takes about a third of the country's imports to feed the paper mills of Lower Thameside. Since 1951 the annual amount entering the country has remained at about the 1937–8 average of two million tons.

*Copper (Unwrought)* (Liverpool, 35·4; London, 26·2; Manchester, 20·5). Although there were fluctuations in pre-war years, London's share (w and v) was on the average slightly over a quarter. From 1946 to 1952 the share was moderately above this fraction, but in 1953 and 1954 it was slightly over a quarter once more, and the quantity of imports into London is nearly always exceeded by that into Liverpool.

*Paper, Paperboard, and Manufactures thereof* (London 24·8).

London's share (w and v) has remained the same before and after the war. Newsprint in rolls and Kraft paper generally account for about half the value of these commodities imported into London, the country's biggest single paper market.

*Machinery and Parts thereof* (*other than Electric*) (London, 22·7; Liverpool, 13·1). From 1947 to 1954 London's share (v) was about a third of the country's imports, with moderate variations from year to year probably due to the very miscellaneous nature of this classification.

*Wheat* (London, 21·6; Liverpool, 16·7; Hull, 10·4). London's share (w and v) has remained the same before and after the war.

*Fresh Fruit* (London, 19·9; Liverpool, 12·9; Southampton, 12·2). London's share (w) has remained rather stable, very slightly over a third before 1939, very slightly under a third since 1946. Variations in value have been moderately greater. In post-war years the quantity of fruit entering the port has been about two-thirds of the pre-war trade. In 1954 oranges were the chief item dealt with in London, accounting for £6·4 million of the port's total; next came bananas, £4·8 million; and apples, £4·4 million.

The berths specializing in unloading bananas are 35 shed, Royal Albert Dock and A shed, Royal Victoria Dock. In addition to berths in the Royal Victoria Dock, new berths and sheds have been provided for the fruit trade in the West India Import Dock, and the fruit imports handled in the Western Dock, London Docks, are only ten minutes by road from Spitalfields Market. Most of the fruit is sold by sample at the London Fruit Exchange, Spitalfields, which saves double handling.

*Raw Rubber* (Liverpool, 24·0; London, 18·1). This trade is shared with Liverpool generally in the ratio of eleven to nine with Liverpool predominating. Before the war, when synthetic rubber was not such an important part of the trade, two-thirds of the imports came into London. Only £1·6 million of the London total for 1954 refers to synthetic rubber imports.

Since rubber is exempt from H.M. Customs Duty, only about half the bales imported into London remain in port warehouses, some in No. 1 Warehouse at London Dock having been brought by barge from Tilbury and the Royal Docks.

*Cereals* (*other than Wheat*) *and Cereal Preparations* (London, 16·8; Liverpool, 16·0; Bristol, 10·5). From 1950 to 1954 London's share (v) was about the same as pre-war years, but only about half to two-thirds of the average pre-war quantity was imported. The chief berths for grain are in the Millwall Dock and along the south side of the Royal Victoria Dock. Grain is also discharged at these and other berths by P.L.A. floating pneumatic grain discharging plants at a maximum rate of 300 tons per hour.

*Cheese* (London, 16·7; Liverpool, 4·3). National imports of this commodity were at a high level in the immediate post-war years when London's storage accommodation problem was most acute. Then as the country's imports declined to about their pre-war level, London's imports increased after 1951 to fall only moderately short of the pre-war trade.

*Hides and Skins* (*Undressed*) (London, 14·1; Liverpool 12·9). London's share (v) shows a great decrease over its pre-war share mainly because of a re-organization of the tanning trade dealing with undressed cattle hides which are now imported chiefly through Liverpool.

In 1954 undressed fur skins accounted for £6·6 million of the London total but only for £1·3 million in Liverpool's trade. London is an international fur market because it is situated about midway between the great north continental fur-bearing regions of the world, because of the prestige in this trade of the Hudson's Bay Company and the fact that at present British processing costs are low.

*Tobacco* (Liverpool, 25·1; Bristol, 17·8; London, 13·8). The high levels of national imports in the immediate post-war years (when much of the increase came to London) later subsided to the pre-war average. London's share (w and v) in 1954 was about the same as pre-war.

About fifty warehouses in London store unmanufactured tobacco, the principal concentration being on the north side of the Royal Victoria Dock. The leaf may stay in bond maturing for up to eighteen months; garbling (separating sound from unsound leaf) and sampling are usually undertaken by the warehouse keepers. About a quarter of the stocks of the United Kingdom are held in bond in the Port of London area, with a duty paid value of about £300 million.

*Vegetable Oils* (London, 13·3; Liverpool, 12·1). Comparing the whole of the post- and pre-war periods, London's share (v) shows a slight decline. The imports into London are of a much greater range than those into Liverpool where palm oil is of over-whelming importance.

*Wines and Spirits* (London, 8·5). London's share (w and v) in post-war years showed a slight decrease on its pre-war share; but in each year since 1952 national imports have been running at only about three-quarters of the annual quantity imported pre-war and in the 1946–51 period. In London the ratio of wines to spirits is about two to one, by value.

Whereas most wines arrive by direct shipment at London Docks, most spirits arrive by barge. Brandy may come from France, Australia, South Africa, Cyprus, or Greece; and rum always arrives in ocean-going vessels. At the London Docks there are ten acres of bonded underground vaults, sufficient to hold 35,000 casks. Many of the vaults in London for storing wines and spirits are found in the arches beneath railways and the main-line railway stations which are raised on viaducts. Many of the London wine importers have their premises between London Docks and the Vintry in Upper Thames Street.

*Imports* (*conclusion*). The most important commodities which are not imported into London in relatively significant quantities are cotton and tin; for imports of copper and rubber the Port of London is usually second in importance to the Port of Liverpool; second to Hull for raw wool; and third to Liverpool and Bristol for tobacco.

EXPORTS

If the year ended March 31, 1954 is compared with the year ended March 31, 1937, the tonnage of exports is seen to have increased to 8,946,301 tons from 5,836,414 tons. This is certainly a result of the change in the character of the national export trade rather than of any special development at London. For example, if the details of the commodities exported are examined, London's share of the national export trade for each commodity has remained remarkably similar from pre-war to post-war. For no commodity does London's average share (v) of the export traffic rise above a slight increase over its pre-war average share. In the case of the export of woollen and worsted yarns and woven

TABLE XXII

*Exports from London, 1954 (worth over £10 million, 1948)*

| Exported Commodity | Value £ million | Percentage of Total U.K. Exports by Value, |
|---|---|---|
| | 1954 | 1954 |
| Road Vehicles and Parts ... ... | 139·5 | 47 |
| Machinery (other than Agricultural and Electric) ... ... ... ... | 130·3 | 32 |
| Electric Machinery, Apparatus, and Appliances ... ... ... ... | 80·6 | 47 |
| Chemicals (including Drugs, Dyes, and Colours) ... ... ... | 68·5 | 34 |
| Vehicles (other than Road) and Parts ... | 49·5 | 32 |
| Postal Packages ... ... ... ... | 25·5 | 30 |
| Refined Sugar ... ... ... ... | 20·3 | 76 |
| Non-ferrous Base Metals (in Alloys) ... | 18·4 | 33 |
| Paper, Paperboard, and Manufactures thereof ... ... ... ... | 18·1 | 54 |
| Iron and Steel and Manufactures thereof | 14·6 | 11 |
| Woollen and Worsted Yarns and Woven Fabrics ... ... ... ... | 11·7 | 14 |
| Cotton Yarns and Woven Fabrics ... | 11·7 | 10 |
| Agricultural Machinery ... ... ... | 5·6 | 35 |
| Total of Exports ... ... | 846·8 | |

fabrics there is even a moderate decrease in London's share (v) of the national trade from 22% to 14%.

The type of goods exported is influenced more by the ports called at overseas by general cargo or passenger/cargo liners than by the situation of the factory in Great Britain. This is to say that the port's foreland (*i.e.* its overseas markets) is a more important factor in the export trade than the port's hinterland.

Evidence for this may be seen under the heading, 'Machinery (other than Agricultural and Electric)', where factories in most parts of England must find their products tabulated, so bewildering is the variety. The chief items are tractors (54,646 exported in 1954, worth £22·3 million), internal combustion engines (£9 million), aeroplane engines (£6·7 million), machine tools (£6·4 million), mechanical handling equipment (£5·5 million), and pumps (£5·4 million). Indeed, machinery in one form or another dominates London's exports, accounting for slightly under half the export trade by value.

The high place in the export list of cotton and woollen yarns and woven fabrics is also an indication of the influence of the foreland predominating over the hinterland. Furthermore, the unexpected item of 'postal packages' emphasizes the superior overseas connections of London; a third of the United Kingdom exported postal packages passes through London, at the rate of 3,330,000 per year.

Since November 1956 factory-to-ship transits have been provided for export traffic from thirty-five industrial centres, as far north as Manchester and Leeds. Under this scheme full rail truck loads of export goods are assured next-morning arrivals at the Royal, and the India and Millwall Docks.

ENTREPOT

The entrepot trade is concerned with imported goods which do not leave the port area and remain unchanged in character, or undergo some simple manipulation in a port warehouse, and which are then exported to foreign destinations. The title of the classification of this type of goods by H.M. Customs is *Exports of Imported Merchandise*.[15]

Entrepot goods are exempted from inward and outward port rates provided that they are so declared within seventy-two hours of ship's report. When some simple operation upon the entrepot goods is required it is performed in a bonded warehouse without payment of duty with the consent of H.M. Customs.

One simpler form of the entrepot trade has not been reintroduced.

'The procedure for Importation and Exportation of Free Goods in transit on Through Bills of Lading (other than goods transhipped under bond) was suspended in 1939 and has not been resumed.'[16]

The entrepot trade has declined relatively from the days when the majority of goods were despatched *on consignment*, when the shipper sold his goods on an overseas market. Now he can have his cargo discharged at several alternative ports as long as he specifies which port before the ship has made her first discharge. More importantly, the growth of shipments against firm orders, or *indents* has militated against entrepot traffic.

In view of the above it is not surprising that the commodities which appear most prominent in London's entrepot trade are those which are dealt with by the London commodity markets.

TABLE XXIII

*Exports of Imported Merchandise, 1954 (worth over £1 million)*

|  | £ million |
|---|---|
| Wool ... ... ... ... ... | 10·0 |
| Tea ... ... ... ... ... | 7·3 |
| Hides and Skins ... ... ... | 5·6 |
| Copper ... ... ... ... ... | 2·8 |
| Coffee ... ... ... ... ... | 2·0 |
| Cocoa ... ... ... ... ... | 1·9 |
| Spices ... ... ... ... ... | 1·9 |
| Rubber ... ... ... ... ... | 1·6 |
| Animal Bristles ... ... ... | 1·4 |
| Wines and Spirits ... ... ... | 1·4 |
| Total (Entrepot) ... ... | 53·4 |

One final general statement on the trade of the port may be permitted. Analysis of the commodity statistics reveals that factors of national policy such as de-rationing, cessation of bulk buying, fostering of the export trade, emergence of 'soft' and 'hard' currency areas, are far more potent in changing the character of the port's trade than any changing factor which is within the port itself or is due to any rivalry with other ports. This is evidence for saying that London is a national port; if the trade of the nation flourishes, so flourishes the nation's port.

## REFERENCES

1. For further details see Sir Oscar Hobson, *How the City Works* (News Chronicle Book, 1955) and *Exchanges and Commodity Markets* (Swiss Bank Corporation, 1955).

2. J. G. Smith, *Organized Produce Markets* (Longmans, 1922).

3. B. S. Yamey, 'Futures Trading in Cocoa, Rubber and Wool Tops', *The Three Banks Review*, 23 (1954), 28–41. To find an acceptable standard in the wool trade it was necessary to use a semi-processed product, wool tops ('Bradford 64s B top' of merino wool), a top being a continuous sliver of combed wool and the raw material of worsted spinning. Dealers in the actuals market of raw wool can hedge in this futures market because the price of the wool tops can be expected to vary in the same way as raw wool. The actuals market in these raw wool tops is in Bradford. Recently, a second wool futures market in 'Bradford 50s carded tops' of crossbred wool has started operations in Plantation House.

4. B. S. Yamey, 'The Metal Exchange', *The Three Banks Review*, 30 (1956), 21–39.

5. O.E., *mynecenu*; M.E., *minchen*: nun. The lane was probably named after a small community of nuns established in this area before the twelfth century.

6. Plantation House was erected in 1936 for the original London Rubber Exchange Ltd., the leaseholder of the premises.

7. The name was chosen to mark the provenance of the original trades in grain, oilseeds, tallow, etc. The ancient coffee-house also had New World interests and was accordingly called 'The Virginia and Baltick'.

8. P.L.A. Information Office and the *Annual Statement of the Trade of the United Kingdom*, Vols. I–IV (H.M. Customs and Excise, H.M.S.O.).

9. 'Transhipment' is here confined to meaning goods transferred from one vessel to another in the foreign or coastwise trade.

10. Imported crude petroleum is however included, although below this figure, because of a phenomenal rise since 1948. As will be seen, the arbitrary figure chosen for goods in the entrepot trade was a value above £1 million in 1954.

11. 'London' includes Leigh, Queenborough, and Rochford in H.M. Customs and Excise returns. Commodities imported from other ports of the United Kingdom are not included; coal imports are discussed in Chapter VI.

12. Statistics for individual ports are published triennially in the *Annual Statement of the Trade of the United Kingdom*, Vol. IV *Supplement* (H.M. Customs and Excise, H.M.S.O.).

13. Based on figures quoted by C. R. Harler, *The Culture and Marketing of Tea* (Oxford University Press, 1956), 231.

14. W. Smith, *The Distribution of Population and the Location of Industry on Merseyside* (Liverpool University Press, 1942), 113.

15. '. . . comprise goods, materials and articles exported in the condition which they were imported, or after having undergone operations which leave them essentially unchanged, e.g. simple blending, cleaning, drying, sorting, husking or shelling, repacking, bottling, &c.' *Annual Statement of the Trade of the United Kingdom, 1954*, General Introductory Notes, 11 (b) (H.M. Customs and Excise, H.M.S.O., 1956). Quoted by permission of the Controller of H.M. Stationery Office.

16. *Ibid.*, 11 (c), quoted by permission of the Controller of H.M. Stationery Office.

M

# CHAPTER IX

## FLOREAT IMPERII PORTUS

In the previous chapters the port has been discussed with reference to its development in time and, more particularly, in space. Such has been the main purpose of this geography of the port. However, having already discussed much of the detail, this concluding chapter will not lose an opportunity of dealing briefly with three topics which refer to the port as a whole: the P.L.A., the Men, and the Port and the Passage of Time.[1]

### THE PORT OF LONDON AUTHORITY

There are thirty board members of the P.L.A., a body corporate by statutory definition composed as follows:

Elected (18):

| | |
|---|---|
| By payers of dues, wharfingers, and owners of river craft ... ... ... ... ... ... ... | 17 |
| By wharfingers ... ... ... ... ... | 1 |

Appointed (10):

| | |
|---|---|
| By the Admiralty ... ... ... ... ... | 1 |
| By the Ministry of Transport ... ... ... | 2[a] |
| By the London County Council (being members of the Council) ... ... ... ... ... ... | 2 |
| By the London County Council (not being members of the Council) ... ... ... ... | 2[a] |
| By the City Corporation (being a member of the Corporation) ... ... ... ... ... | 1 |
| By the City Corporation (not being a member of the Corporation) ... ... ... ... ... | 1 |
| By the Trinity House ... ... ... ... | 1 |
| Total ... ... ... ... ... ... | 28 |

Chairman ⎱ elected by above, and may be drawn from
Vice-Chairman ⎰ outside their number.

At first glance it appears anomalous that the wharfingers should be represented on the board of their rivals. However, two points must be remembered: the P.L.A. is concerned not only with administration of dock systems but also with the maintenance and efficiency of the river highway, of vital interest to all in the port; secondly, with long established rate agreements and a traditional division of traffic, the competition between public authority and private interest is greatly attenuated. Of the twenty-eight ordinary members, those elected by the users of the port have a majority of eight. This seems right, because these users benefit by adequate development of facilities, while, as payers of dues, they resist inefficient management and wasteful expenditure.[3]

Much of the credit for the success of the P.L.A. from the beginning belongs to Lord Devonport (1856–1934), the first chairman until 1925. He had also been the principal pilot of the *Port of London* Bill when Parliamentary Secretary to the Board of Trade under Lloyd George in the Liberal Government of 1906.

The main sources of revenue for the P.L.A. are charges on goods (39·9%); charges, dues, etc. on vessels (25·5%); and port rates on goods[4] (15·8%) which helped to make up a revenue of £14,936,070 in the year ended March 31, 1954. Operating expenses accounted for half this income; maintenance (11·8%), interest on port stock (7·4%), deferred repairs (5·2%), and dredging (4·6%) were the next costliest items in the same year.

The head offices of the P.L.A. (*see* front endpaper) are at Trinity Square on the site of the former Crutched Friars Warehouse of the London and St. Katharine Docks Company.

### THE MEN

Nobody would wish to present a merely mechanistic picture of the port; but dock labour is a difficult subject to treat briefly, especially within the context of a single port, because much of its history can only be understood in a national setting. The subject is also complicated by many considerations outside the scope of this book. A most useful summary of the history of dock labour up to a recent date has been provided by A. H. J. Bown and C. A. Dove.[5]

The following table shows how the labour force has decreased.

More trade has been handled by fewer registered dock workers. Decasualization, more machines, and more piecework have contributed to this desirable state of affairs. London has about 35% of the dock workers of the United Kingdom who handle about the same proportion of the national trade, by value.

TABLE XXIV

*Dock Workers*[6]

| | Census of Average Daily Port Employment in the London Area | Number entered on Register of Dock Workers in the London Area | National Total on Register of Dock Workers |
|---|---|---|---|
| 1921 ... | 34,000[7] | — | — |
| 1924 ... | 31,000[7] | — | — |
| 1925 ... | — | 55,000[7] | — |
| 1931 ... | 26,000[7] | 36,000[7] | — |
| 1938 ... | — | 43,000[8] | 130,000[9] |
| 1949 ... | — | 26,798[10] | 74,850[10] |
| 1955 ... | — | 31,448[10] | 80,577[10] |

The internal river traffic of the port is carried on by about 4,200 tugmen and lightermen.

THE PORT AND THE PASSAGE OF TIME

To remark that some installations of the Port of London are old and ought to be abandoned is to be superficial. How surprised Thomas Telford would be to see his warehouses at the St. Katharine Docks still actively used, well over a hundred years after their erection ; and D. A. Alexander's warehouses at London Dock are over 150 years old. In such a large organization which has existed over such a long period of time, one must expect to find some features which are very old, still used but almost due for replacement, cheek by jowl with modern installations. The annual trade statistics may show a steady progression through the years, but this work of the port is only achieved through the continual change of its parts.

'Other examples are all round us. The wood which looks today much as it looked when we were children is none the less largely a new wood. . . . An economy [or a port] is an example of a process of the same kind. . . . Viewed as a whole the system may maintain a steady state, in that there may be no change in the total effort which goes in, the total product which comes out . . . but this . . . would be achieved only by . . . continuous change within.'[11]

In any long-established wood there are bound to be some very old trees. The long life of port installations

'is made economically feasible by a gradual down grading made possible by the range in the size of ship required for trading purposes.'[12]

In P.L.A. engineering an average life of fifty years is assumed.[13] Docks and dock installations have to be built robustly to discharge their functions efficiently. This presents a problem for the port engineer when designing for special handling. Should he design a structure adapted to present specialized needs with a limited life in view and how long should this be? Or should he design for general cargo as well as for the special handling techniques, the latter being easily removed if conditions change during the long life of the structure? The latter policy is generally adopted.[14]

If mobile cranes and fork lift trucks are to be the tools around which quay mechanization is to be developed, the present method of designing high transit sheds, high doors, and as few stanchions as possible is to build ably for the future. Should the increasing quay mechanization require greater distance between quay wall and transit shed, the Port of London may face a serious internal handicap. Many 'peninsular' areas between docks restrict expansion. Both in the docks and along the riverside are many areas where other built-up property presses close outside the dock and warehouse walls and also presses warehouses and transit sheds closer to the quay walls and the riverside than perhaps future generations would like.

As far as ship berths, lock entrances, and river channels are concerned, port authorities should anticipate the development of shipping likely to use them. Ideally, when the shipping company approves a new and larger vessel for a certain route, the port which hopes to receive the vessel should already have, or have under construction, channels of approach and installations of a sufficient size to cope with the vessel. Such is the background to the construction of the new berth in Tilbury Dock for new 40,000-ton vessels coming into the Tilbury-Sydney service within the next decade.

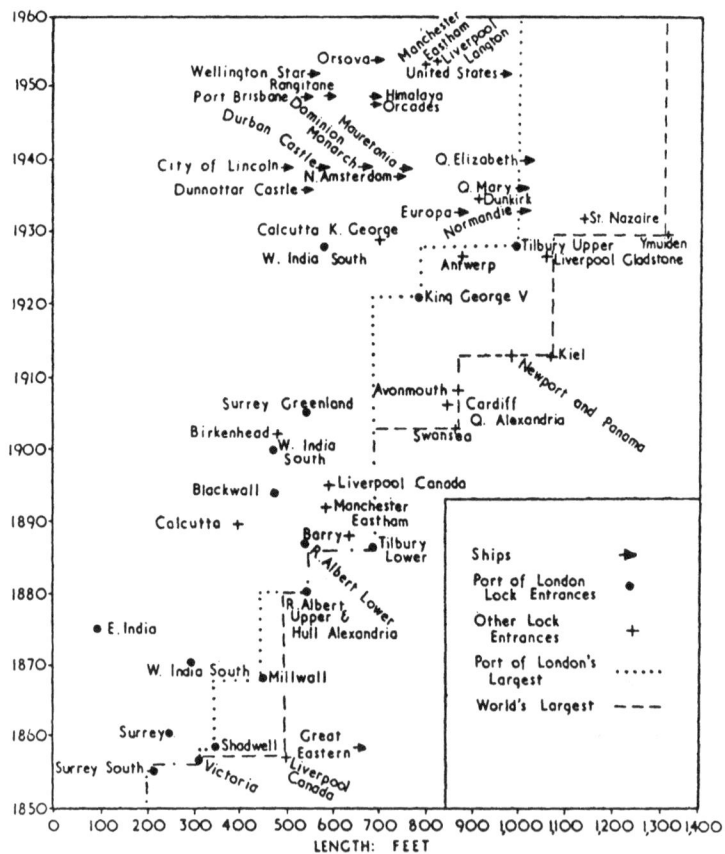

FIG. 14.—Lengths of Port Entrance Locks and of Ships.

After W. P. Shepherd-Baron (1954), by kind permission of the P.L.A. and of the Institution of Civil Engineers.

Limiting dimensions for lock entrances are length, width or beam, and depth at H.W.S.T. Figure 14 shows that the length of the locks of the Port of London have provided a good margin at the date of their construction. The King George V and Tilbury Upper Locks were constructed under the aegis of the P.L.A. with ample foresight. Sir Frederick Palmer, the first P.L.A. Chief Engineer, expressed his fear of repeating the former mistake of building entrances too short for future requirements. Only the *Queen Mary* and *Queen Elizabeth* are too long to use the docks. The *Mauretania* (35,677 tons gross) was built to conform with the dimensions of the King George V entrance lock and has used it once. The *Dominion Monarch* (27,155 tons gross) is the largest vessel to use this lock regularly. The same two 'Queen' liners are also too wide for the entrance locks, but all commercial vessels could use the port if depth alone were the only limiting factor.[15] This emphasizes the wonderful channel of access constructed in the river by the P.L.A.

DEFINITION OF THE PORT OF LONDON

In the first chapter it was pointed out that it was impossible to define the areas which make up the port by any inherent similarity of form. Nor are the areas continuous. For example, the P.L.A. Head Offices building in Trinity Square is physically divorced from the dock systems and the river that it administers; the vital links are by mail and telephone and through the movements of the chief officers of the P.L.A. organization. From the survey reported in the previous chapters, it is apparent that the definition must include the following chief constituents which together *function* as the Port of London.

A. Tidal Thames, Teddington to Sea Reach Buoy No. 1 (see Fig. 1).
B. Lower Lea (south of Hackney Marshes); eastern two miles of Grand Union Canal; Limehouse Cut; and other waterways close to their confluence with the tidal Thames.
C. Dock Systems.
D. River Traffic.

E. P.L.A. Head Offices.

F. City Commodity Markets.

G. Thameside Industries.

H. Inland Warehouses controlled by the P.L.A. or Wharfingers.

The code letters of the above list (A–H) are inserted after the appropriate section of the following definition.

*The Port of London comprises those areas of the Tidal Thames (A) and its contiguous rivers and waterways (B), and dock systems (C) where the each-way exchange between land and water transport (D) can be observed; together with other inland installations which control this activity (E, F) or are vitally dependent upon it (G, H).*[16]

R. S. MacElwee defined a port as a harbour with terminal facilities, and the harbour is

'a body of water protected from wind and wave action with water of sufficient depth and with bottom of good holding ground so that vessels may find haven in it and anchor safely.'[17]

Following this definition, the harbour of the Port of London is therefore the tidal Thames and the wet docks; F. W. Morgan (1952) has pointed out that the harbour is partly natural and in part artificial where the river has been dredged and in the wet docks.[18]

Nobody has successfully defined the Port of London's hinter-land. This has developed until for some commodities it embraces most of Great Britain, because the port is so large in such a small island. For some foodstuffs the port is merely the larder door for Greater London. A separate hinterland needs to be worked out for each class of goods. Such studies would have to concentrate more on the particular commodities rather than on the port through which they pass.

The sizes of the port's land and water sites have greatly expanded with time. Similarly, the situation of the port is no longer confined to the context of the London Basin but is rather the North Sea Lowlands, a situation shared by other ports on the continent of Europe which are rivals for some traffic, especially that of an entrepot variety.

CONCLUSION

'Is the Port of London efficient when compared with other major ports?' There is no simple answer. A port may be efficient at handling one type of cargo, less efficient with another; general cargo takes longer to deal with than bulk cargo. A port is unique like its own tide. The comparison may be pushed further. Each coastal tide is the product of dynamic lunar and solar forces acting upon the sea over the relatively static outline of submarine morphology and the coastline. Each port is the product of its tide, submarine morphology, and the coastline, and the reaction of the genius of the men at the place to serve the hinterland of their port and its foreland overseas. A Parliamentary Committee or a Royal Commission, not a geographer, is competent to answer the question of the port's efficiency.

There have been two periods in the port's history when the answer was an emphatic 'No!' Firstly, at the end of the eighteenth century the quays of the port could not cope with the goods imported; and, secondly, at the beginning of this century, the river could not cope with the draught of vessels wishing to reach the port. Fortunately, the steps recommended by a Select Committee and a Royal Commission to remedy these defects were in each case supremely right. The solution to the first problem was found in the construction of the wet docks. The second problem was solved with the inception of the P.L.A., whose greatest single contribution has been the excavation and maintenance of a river channel of sufficient depth for all ships wishing to use the port.

Only one subject of criticism will be dealt with here, in a constructive spirit. The road approaches of the port could be improved.

Downstream from Tower Bridge the river traffic of the port has precluded the erection of another bridge. There are only two road tunnels, at Rotherhithe and Blackwall, and two ferries, at Woolwich and Tilbury. Only those who have used these routes know of the frustrating delays involved and the carbon monoxide nightmare of tunnels designed in the nineteenth century. Those who cross the river by road vehicle east of London, unless they do so underground at night, are obliged to have an elastic conception of time. The port suffers from the lack of easy approach to its docks and wharves and the difficulty of movement to the full circle of its hinterland. Undoubtedly, the right of way enjoyed by the port's river traffic has contributed to the north-south barrier which the river presents to road traffic.

The Blackwall Tunnel duplication scheme, with an estimated cost of £7·7 million, cannot be brought within the early years of the road programme.[19] The Dartford-Purfleet Road Tunnel is long overdue. When it is opened in 1962 it is estimated that two million vehicles will use it every year; but in the next five to six years the traffic demands of the developing port and its associated industries will increase this figure. This 'head' of demand by cross-river traffic amounting to two million vehicles per annum is dramatic evidence of part of the shackles borne by road traffic near Lower Thameside. The tonnage of export goods coming to the port by rail was 25% greater in 1955 than in 1937; the corresponding figure for road transport was nearly 275%.[20] A further tunnel at Woolwich might solve the problems, replacing the very efficient but badly overworked Free Ferry. Pier Road, North Woolwich and Hare Street, Woolwich, might then become approaches to the river instead of parking places for the ferry queues.

The tortuous course of Manor Way, east of the Royal Docks, with its two bascule bridges ought to be replaced by a more direct route as a counterpart to the splendid Silvertown Way west of the docks.[21] The problem of this route will become more difficult if and when the new dock is constructed north of the Royal Albert Dock. A bold solution might be the combination of a new road and the northern approaches to a Woolwich Tunnel.

Finally, in the case of the London and St. Katharine Docks, built before the railways, an extra heavy burden is placed on road transport. A comprehensive plan is necessary to relieve congestion in the approach roads, especially near the main entrance.

Of course, these schemes must be weighed against other needs, but is it often borne in mind that in these cases not only would road congestion be alleviated but the working of our greatest port most materially assisted? Great expense is undoubtedly involved, but there is an American saying: 'We pay for good roads whether we have them or not, but we pay more if we don't have them.'

It is perhaps significant that the one criticism ventured here is concerned with land communications. The water situation and site of the port are now more magnificent that when first taken advantage of by the Romans. Dredging has increased the worth of the river, but all those past and present who have built up this great port would admit the splendid natural advantages of the Thames.

This was the opinion of the Royal Commission of 1902. Let part of their concluding paragraph stand as the concluding paragraph of this book, to be followed by the house motto of the P.L.A. that they so wisely set up, with its embodied wish warmly echoed here: 'May the Imperial Port Prosper!'

'In conclusion, we desire to say that our inquiry into the conditions of the Port of London has convinced us of its splendid natural advantages. Among these are the geographical position of the Port; the magnitude, wealth and energy of the population behind it; the fine approach from the sea; the river tides strong enough to transport traffic easily to all parts, yet not so violent as to make navigation difficult; [and] land along the shores suitable for dock construction and all commercial purposes . . .'

*'Floreat imperii portus'*

## REFERENCES

1. For more details of other topics see the alphabetical list of references, notably under L. Gordon (1937) and H. Le Mesurier (1934), for P.L.A. constitution and administration; under W. P. Shepherd-Baron (1954) and G. A. Wilson (1953), for dock engineering and dock installations; under E. S. Tooth (1955), for ship discharge; and under A. H. J. Bown and C. A. Dove (1950) for port administration and operation.

2. One of each represents labour.

3. L. Gordon, 'The Port of London Authority', *Public Enterprise*, edited by W. A. Robson (Allen & Unwin, 1937), 23. H. S. Morrison, *How London is Governed* (People's Universities

Press, 1949), while agreeing with this, holds that it is wrong that private interests should dominate a public authority and has described the P.L.A. as a 'capitalist soviet'.

4. Transhipment goods, bunker coal and fuel oil, goods carried in certain vessels to and from the rivers Medway and Swale, and fresh fish are exempt from these rates. Incidentally, the revenue derived from port rates on goods was not available to the nineteenth-century dock companies.

5. A. H. J. Bown and C. A. Dove, *Port Administration and Operation* (Chapman and Hall, 1950), Chapter VII, give a brief history up to the *Dock Workers (Regulation of Employment) Order*, 1947. A. H. J. Bown, *Port Economics* (The Dock and Harbour Authority, 1953), carries the story further. For accounts of post-war strikes and stoppages, and for later details about the Dock Workers Scheme see *Report of a Committee of Inquiry into Unofficial Stoppages in the London Docks* (Cmd. 8236, H.M.S.O., 1951) and *Report of a Committee appointed on 27th July, 1955, to inquire into the operation of the Dock Workers (Regulation of Employment) Scheme* (Cmd. 9813, H.M.S.O., 1956).

6. For the distinction between 'dock worker' and other trades and professions in the docks see A. H. J. Bown and C. A. Dove *vide supra*, 202. Inclusion of all such workers in the table would about double the figures.

7. *New Survey of London Life and Labour* (King, 1931), Vol. ii, 399–402.

8. D. L. Munby, *Industry and Planning in Stepney* (Oxford University Press, 1951), 316.

9. A. H. J. Bown, 'Ports and Shipping Turn-Round: Causes of Delay and Suggested Remedies', *The Dock and Harbour Authority*, 33 (1953), 264.

10. Registered labour forces at the last week of each year, National Dock Labour Board Statistical Officer.

11. Sir Geoffrey Vickers, in a talk broadcast on December 23, 1955, and published in *The Listener*, December 29, 1955.

12. *Report by the British National Committee of the Permanent International Association of Navigational Congresses.* 'Depths to be provided in Seaport Entrance Channels and Berths,' Excerpt from Bulletin, 42 (1955).

13. G. A. Wilson, 'Port of London Authority Engineering Works,

1952', *Proceedings of the Institution of Civil Engineers*, 2, II (1953), 556.

14. N. N. B. Ordman, 'The Port of London. Some Engineering Aspects of Post-war Reconstruction and Development', *The Dock and Harbour Authority*, 33 (1952), 135–6.

15. W. P. Shepherd Baron, 'The Docks of London', *Proceedings of the Institution of Civil Engineers*, 3 (1954), Figs. 4, Plate 2. See also the *Report by the British National Committee of the Permanent International Association of Navigational Congresses, 1955, op. cit.*, for general reflections on changing dimensions of ships and port facilities.

16. This definition may be compared with the statutory definition quoted as the Appendix.

17. *Encyclopaedia of the Social Sciences* (MacMillan, 1934), Vol. 12, 255.

18. Page 49.

19. Part of the scheme may be started shortly. This is the reconstruction of the northern approach to the Blackwall Tunnel with a flyunder to take the approach road under the East India Dock Road to which it will be connected by semi-clover leaf link roads.

20. *Third Report of the Ports Efficiency Committee to the Minister of Transport and Civil Aviation* (H.M.S.O., 1956).

21. On May 22, 1956, the Minister of Housing and Local Government announced approval of a development plan by West Ham Borough Council which includes progressive construction of a Docks Relief Road northwards from the existing Silvertown Way.

## STATUTORY DEFINITION OF THE PORT OF LONDON

'Description of the Limits of the Port of London

The limits of the Port of London shall commence at an imaginary straight line (in this Act referred to as "the landward limit of the Port of London") drawn from high-water mark on the bank of the River Thames at the boundary line between the parishes of Teddington and Twickenham in the county of Middlesex to high-water mark on the Surrey bank of the river immediately opposite the first-mentioned point and extend down both sides of the River Thames to an imaginary straight line (in this Act referred to as "the seaward limit of the Port of London") drawn from the pilot mark at the entrance of Havengore Creek in the county of Essex to the Land's End at Warden Point in the Isle of Sheppey in the county of Kent and shall include all islands rivers streams creeks waters watercourses channels harbours docks and places within the before-mentioned limits and all places which under any Act of Parliament are to be deemed within the Port of London but shall not include any part of the River Medway above the seaward limit of the jurisdiction of the conservators of the River Medway or any part of the River Swale or any part of the River Lee or Bow Creek within the jurisdiction of the Lee Conservancy Board or any part of the Grand Junction Canal.'

*Port of London (Consolidation) Act*, 1920, First Schedule.

# ALPHABETICAL LIST OF REFERENCES[1]

ABERCROMBIE, Sir Patrick. *Greater London Plan*. H.M.S.O., 1944.

ADDISON, W. *English Fairs and Markets*. Batsford, 1953.

——. *Thames Estuary*. Hale, 1954.

ALLEN, F. H. 'The Thames Model Investigation', *The Dock and Harbour Authority*, 32 (1952), 373–8.

—— and J. GRINDLEY. 'Radioactive Tracers in the Thames Estuary', *The Dock and Harbour Authority*, 37 (1957), 302–6.

——, W. A. PRICE, and SIR CLAUDE INGLIS. 'Model Experiments on the Storm Surge of 1953 in the Thames Estuary and the Reduction of Future Surges', *Proceedings of the Institution of Civil Engineers*, 4 (1955), 48–82.

*Annual Statement of the Trade of the United Kingdom*, Vols. I–IV. H.M. Customs and Excise, H.M.S.O.

ATTON, H., and H. H. HOLLAND. *The King's Customs*. 2 vols. Murray, 1910.

BELL, A. *Port of London 1909–34*. P.L.A., 1934.

——. *The Said Noble River*. P.L.A., 1937.

BELLOC, H. *The Historic Thames*. Dent, 1907.

——. *The River of London*. Foulis, 1912.

BINNS, A. 'The Thames and its Docks', *Transactions of the Institution of Engineers-in-Charge*, 42 (1936–7), 124–40.

——. 'Mainly Port of London', *Proceedings of the Institution of Mechanical Engineers*, 144 (1940), 50–3.

BIRD, J. 'The Industrial Development of Lower Thameside', *Geography*, XXXVII (1952), 89–96.

BOWEN, F. C. *The Port of London*. Dryden, 1948.

——. *Port of London Guide*. Coram, 1955.

BOWN, A. H. J. 'Ports and Shipping Turn-Round: Causes of Delay and Suggested Remedies', *The Dock and Harbour Authority*, 33 (1953), 264–7, 270.

[1] The place of the publication of books is London unless otherwise stated. *Reports* are arranged chronologically together under the word *Report*.

BOWN, A. H. J. *Port Economics*. The Dock and Harbour Authority, 1953.

—— and C. A. DOVE. *Port Administration and Operation*. Chapman & Hall, 1950.

BRETT-JAMES, N. G. 'Precincts and Trade Quarters : a History of Use-zones in the City of London', *Architectural Review*, 100 (1946), 129–50.

BROMEHEAD, C. E. N. 'The Influence of Its Geography on the Growth of London', *Geographical Journal*, LX (1922), 125–35.

BROODBANK, Sir Joseph. *History of the Port of London*. 2 vols. O'Connor, 1921.

CAPPER, C. *The Port and Trade of London*. Smith, Elder, 1862.

(*The*) *City of London : a Record of Destruction and Survival* (Improvements and Town Planning Committee of the Corporation of London). Architectural Press, 1950.

COLEMAN, A. 'Landscape and Planning in Relation to the Cement Industry of Thames-side', *Town Planning Review*, XXV (1954), 216–30.

COLQUHOUN, P. *A Treatise on the Commerce and Police of the River Thames*. 1800.

CORNISH, V. *The Great Capitals : an Historical Geography*. Methuen, 1923.

(*Administrative*) *County of London Development Plan 1951 : Analysis*. London County Council, 1951.

COURSE, A. G. *The Place of Tilbury in the Port of London*. P.L.A. MS, 1946.

CRACKNELL, B. E. 'The Lower Thames and Medway Petroleum Industry', *Geography*, XXXVII (1952), 79–88.

——. *The Alluvial Marshlands of the Lower Thames Estuary*. Unpublished thesis, Ph.D. University of London, 1953.

CRITCHELL, J. T., and J. RAYMOND. *A History of the Frozen Meat Trade*. Constable, 1912.

CROUCH, A. P. *Silvertown and Neighbourhood*. Burleigh, 1900.

CUNNINGHAM, B. *The Estuarial Embankments of the River Thames*. Report to the XVIth Congress of Navigation, Brussels, 1935.

(*The*) *Dock and Harbour Authority*. Monthly, 1920 to date.

DOWLING, S. W. *The Exchanges of London*. Butterworth, 1929.

DUGDALE, Sir William. *History of Imbanking and Draining*. 2nd Edition, 1772.

ELLIS, A. *Three Hundred Years on London River: the Hay's Wharf Story, 1651–1951*. Bodley Head, 1952.

ELMES, J. *A Scientific, Historical and Commercial Survey of the Harbour and Port of London*. Weale, 1838.

*Exchanges and Commodity Markets*. Swiss Bank Corporation, 1955.

FALLON, T. *River Police*. Muller, 1956.

FISHER, J. A. 'Reconstruction of the Gallions Lower Entrance Lock at the Royal Docks of the Port of London Authority', *Proceedings of the Institution of Civil Engineers*, 5 (1956), 136–69.

FORSHAW, J. H., and SIR PATRICK ABERCROMBIE. *County of London Plan*. Macmillan, 1943.

FOSTER, Sir William. *East London*. Historical Association Pamphlet No. 100. Bell, 1935.

GORDON, L. 'The Port of London Authority', *Public Enterprise*, edited by W. A. Robson, 13–57. Allen & Unwin, 1937.

GREEN, A. F. 'The Problem of London's Drainage', *Geography*, XLI (1956), 147–54.

HALL, W. B. *The Origin and History of Trinity High Water*. MS. Report to the P.L.A., 1939.

HARLER, C. R. *The Culture and Marketing of Tea*. Oxford University Press, 1956.

HARRIS, C. D. 'Electricity Generation in London, England', *Geographical Review*, XXXI (1941), 127–34.

HERBERT, J. *The Port of London*. Collins, 1947.

HICKMAN, G. M. *The Origins and Changing Functions of Settlement in South-east London, with Special Reference to the Flood-plain Section of the Borough of Deptford*. Unpublished thesis, Ph.D. University of London, 1951.

HOBSON, Sir Oscar. *How the City Works*. News Chronicle Book, 1955.

HOME, G. *Old London Bridge*. Bodley Head, 1931.

HOON, E. E. *The Organization of the English Customs System 1696–1786*, Chapter IV. New York: Appleton-Century, 1938.

HUGH-JONES, E. M. 'Wholesale Food Markets', *The New Survey of London Life and Labour*, Vol. V, II, Chapter III, 115–36. King, 1933.

JONES, L. R. *The Geography of London River*. Methuen, 1931.

KENNEDY, D., and H. E. ALDINGTON. 'Royal Docks Approaches

Improvement, London', *Journal of the Institution of Civil Engineers*, 2 (1935–6), 4–48.

KING, W. B. R., and K. P. OAKLEY. 'The Pleistocene Succession in the Lower Part of the Thames Valley', *Proceedings of the Prehistoric Society*, 2 (1936), 52–76.

KIRKPATRICK, Sir Cyril. 'The Tidal Thames', *Minutes of Proceedings of the Institution of Civil Engineers*, 233 (1931–2), 2–34.

LE MESURIER, H. *The Law relating to the Port of London Authority*. Butterworth, 1934.

LETHABY, W. R. *Londinium, Architecture and the Crafts*. Duckworth, 1923.

LIDDELL, R. R. 'Improvements at the Royal Docks, Port of London Authority', *Journal of the Institution of Civil Engineers*, 10 (1938–9), 283–330.

LINNEY, A. G. *Peepshow of the Port of London*. Sampson Low, 1930.

——. *Lure and Lore of London River*. Sampson Low, 1932.

*London Wharves and Docks*. [Directory] Temple Press, 1954.

LONGFIELD, T. E. *The Subsidence of London*. Paper read to the British Association for the Advancement of Science, York, 1932. Professional Papers, New Series, No. 14. H.M.S.O., 1932.

MACELWEE, R. S. *Ports and Terminal Facilities*. New York: McGraw-Hill, 1918.

MAUGHAN, C. *Markets of London*. Pitman, 1931.

*(The) Metropolitan Borough of Woolwich*. Woolwich Borough Council, 1949.

MORGAN, F. W. *Ports and Harbours*. Hutchinson's University Series, 1952.

MORRISON, H. S. *How London is Governed*. People's Universities Press, 1949.

MUNBY, D. L. *Industry and Planning in Stepney*. Oxford University Press, 1951.

ORDMAN, N. N. B. 'The Port of London. Some Engineering Aspects of Post-war Reconstruction and Development', *The Dock and Harbour Authority*, 33 (1952), 131–6, 170–2.

ORMSBY, H. *London on the Thames*. Sifton, Praed, 1924.

OWEN, Sir David. *The Port of London, Yesterday and Today*. P.L.A., 1927.

OWEN, Sir David. *The Origin and Development of the Ports of the United Kingdom*. Allman, 1948.

PAGE, W. *London: Its Origin and Early Development*. Constable, 1923.

PAILING, K. B. *Planning Problems of London's Waterside Areas*. Unpublished thesis presented for the Diploma in Planning, 1952. [Copy held at L.C.C., County Hall.]

PASSINGHAM, W. J. *London's Markets: their Origin and History*. Sampson, Low. 1935.

PEACOCK, T. B. *P.L.A. Railways*. Locomotive Publishing, 1952.

PELHAM, R. A. 'Medieval Foreign Trade: Eastern Ports', *An Historical Geography of England before 1800*, edited by H. C. Darby, Chapter VII, 298–329. Cambridge University Press, 1951.

PHILLIPS, H. *The Thames about 1750*. Collins, 1951.

POLLARD, S. 'The Decline of Shipbuilding on the Thames', *Economic History Review*, III (1950), 72–89.

*P.L.A. Monthly*. 1925 to date.

POUNDS, N. J. G. 'Port and Outport in North-west Europe', *Geographical Journal*, CIX (1947), 216–28.

POWER, E., and M. M. POSTAN. *Studies in English Trade in the Fifteenth Century*. Routledge, 1933.

PREDDY, W. S. 'The Mixing and Movement of Water in the Estuary of the Thames', *Journal of the Marine Biological Association*, 33 (1954), 645–62.

RASMUSSEN, S. E. *London: the Unique City*. Cape, 1937.

RAWSTRON, E. M. 'The Distribution and Location of Steam-Driven Power Stations in Great Britain', *Geography*, XXXVI (1951), 249–62.

——. 'The Salient Geographical Features of Electricity Production in Great Britain', *Advancement of Science*, VII (1955), 73–82.

——. 'Changes in the Geography of Electricity Production', *Geography*, XL (1955), 92–7.

REES, H. 'A Growth Map for North-east London during the Railway Age', *Geographical Review*, XXXV (1945), 458–65.

*Report from the Committee appointed to enquire into the Best Mode of providing Sufficient Accommodation for the Increased Trade and Shipping of the Port of London*. 1796.

*Report from the Select Committee appointed to consider Evidence taken on Bills for the Improvement of the Port of London*. 1799.

198     ALPHABETICAL LIST OF REFERENCES

*Report of the Select Committee on the State of London Bridge.* 1821.

*Report from the Select Committee on the Port of London.* 1836.

*Report of the Select Committee on Thames Conservancy.* 1863.

*Report of His Majesty's Commissioners Appointed to inquire into the Subject of the Administration of the Port of London and other Matters Connected therewith.* Cd. 1151, H.M.S.O., 1902.

*Report of a Committee appointed at a Conference of Public Authorities to consider the Question of Floods from the River Thames in the County of London.* Cmd. 3045, H.M.S.O., 1928.

*(Joint) Report of Sir George Humphreys and Mr. [later Sir] Frederick Palmer on the Future Standard of Thames Flood Prevention Works in the County of London.* London County Council, 1929.

*Report of the Departmental Committee on Thames Flood Prevention.* Cmd. 4452, H.M.S.O., 1933.

*Reports by Docks and Inland Waterways Executive on Review of Trade Harbours 1948–50.* British Transport Commission, 1951.

*Report of the Departmental Committee on Coastal Flooding.* Cmd. 9165, H.M.S.O., 1954.

*Report by the British National Committee of the Permanent International Association of Navigational Congresses,* 'Depths to be provided in Seaport Entrance Channels and Berths'. Excerpt from Bulletin, 42 (1955).

*(Third) Report of the Ports Efficiency Committee to the Minister of Transport and Civil Aviation.* H.M.S.O., 1956.

*River Thames Wharf Directory.* Gaselee, 1954.

ROBINSON, A. H. W. 'The Changing Navigation Routes of the Thames Estuary', *Journal of the Institute of Navigation*, IV (1951), 357–70.

——. *The Thames Estuary: a Regional Hydrographic Study.* Unpublished thesis, M.Sc. University of London, 1952.

——. 'The Submarine Morphology of Certain Port Approach Systems', *Journal of the Institute of Navigation*, IX (1956), 20–46.

ROLT, L. T. C. 'Samuel Williams & Sons Ltd. 1855–1955', *A Company's Story in its Setting*, 41–86. Williams, 1955.

ROSE, M. *The East End of London.* Cresset, 1951.

SHANKLAND, E. C. *The Thames Estuary and the Port of London: Channel Development by Dredging.* Paper read at the XVIIth International Navigation Congress, Lisbon, 1949.

SHARAN, J. *Marketing of Tea in the United Kingdom 1939–52.* Unpublished thesis, M.Sc. (Econ.). University of London, 1954.

SHEPHERD-BARON, W. P. 'The Docks of London', *Proceedings of the Institution of Civil Engineers*, 3 (1954), 12–42.

SINCLAIR, R. *East London.* Hale, 1950.

SMITH, J. G. *Organized Produce Markets.* Longmans, 1922.

SPATE, O. H. K. 'The Growth of London, A.D. 1660–1800', *An Historical Geography of England before 1800*, edited by H. C. Darby, Chapter XIV, 529–47. Cambridge University Press, 1951.

SPENCE, G. *Nautical Description of Banks and Channels.* 1804.

SPURRELL, F. C. J. 'Early Sites and Embankments on the Margins of the Thames Estuary', *Archaeological Journal*, XLII (1885), 269–302.

——. 'Account of an Excursion to Higham', *Proceedings of the Geologists' Association*, 2 (1889–90), lxxii–lxxiv.

——. 'On the Estuary of the Thames and its Alluvium', *ut supra*, 210–28.

STENTON, F. M. *Norman London.* Historical Association Leaflets, 93–4. Bell, 1934.

STERN, W. M. 'The First London Dock Boom and the Growth of the West India Docks', *Economica*, XIX (1952), 59–77.

STEWART, B. *The Library and the Picture Collection of the Port of London Authority.* Richards, 1955.

STOCKS, G. R. 'Free Trade Zones and Re-Export Reliefs', *The Dock and Harbour Authority*, 27 (1946), 137–8.

'(The) Storm Floods of 1st February, 1953' [a symposium], *Geography*, XXXVIII (1953), 132–89.

STOW, J. *A Survey of London, 1603.* 2 vols. Edited by C. L. Kingsford. Oxford: Clarendon, 1908.

THOMAN, R. S. 'Foreign Trade Zones of the United States', *Geographical Review*, XLII (1952), 631–45.

THOMPSON, A. G. *The Romance of London River.* Bradley, 1934.

——. *The Thames from Tower to Tilbury.* Bradley, 1939.

——. 'Port of London', *World Ports*, 15 (1953), 32–45.

THOMPSON, R. *The Chronicles of Old London Bridge by an Antiquary.* 1839.

TOMLINSON, H. M. *London River.* Cassell, 1951.

Tooth, E. S. *Some Modern Trends in Cargo Handling.* P.L.A., 1955.

Tull, G. J. D. *Some Observations from a Legal Point of View about the River Thames in the Port of London.* P.L.A., 1956.

Vallance, A. *The Centre of the World.* Hodder & Stoughton, 1935.

Vaughan, W. *On Wet Docks, Quays, and Warehouses for the Port of London, with Hints respecting Trade.* 1793.

Wheble, C. L. *The London Lighterage Trade : Its History, Organization and Economics.* Unpublished thesis, M.Sc. (Econ.), University of London, 1939.

Wheeler, R. E. M. [now Sir Mortimer]. 'Introduction', *Report of the Royal Commission on Historical Monuments, 3, Roman London* (1928), 1–67.

Williams, H. *South London.* Hale, 1949.

Wilson, G. A. 'Port of London Authority Engineering Works, 1952', *Proceedings of the Institution of Civil Engineers*, 2, II (1953), 551–604.

Wilson, G., and H. Grace. 'Settlement of London due to Under-drainage of the London Clay', *Journal of the Institution of Civil Engineers*, 19 (1942–3), 100–27.

Wooding, J. W. *As to the Origin and Meaning of 'Trinity High Water' and its Evaluation to Ordnance Datum, Newlyn.* Mimeographed. P.L.A., 1943.

Wooldridge, S. W. *The Geographer as Scientist.* Nelson, 1956.

—— and G. E. Hutchings. *London's Countryside.* Methuen, 1957.

—— and D. L. Linton. *Structure, Surface and Drainage in South-east England.* Philip, 1955.

Yamey, B. S. 'Futures Trading in Cocoa, Rubber and Wool Tops', *The Three Banks Review*, 23 (1954), 28–41.

——. 'The Metal Exchange', *The Three Banks Review*, 30 (1956), 21–39.

# INDEX

Major references are indicated by bold-face numerals.

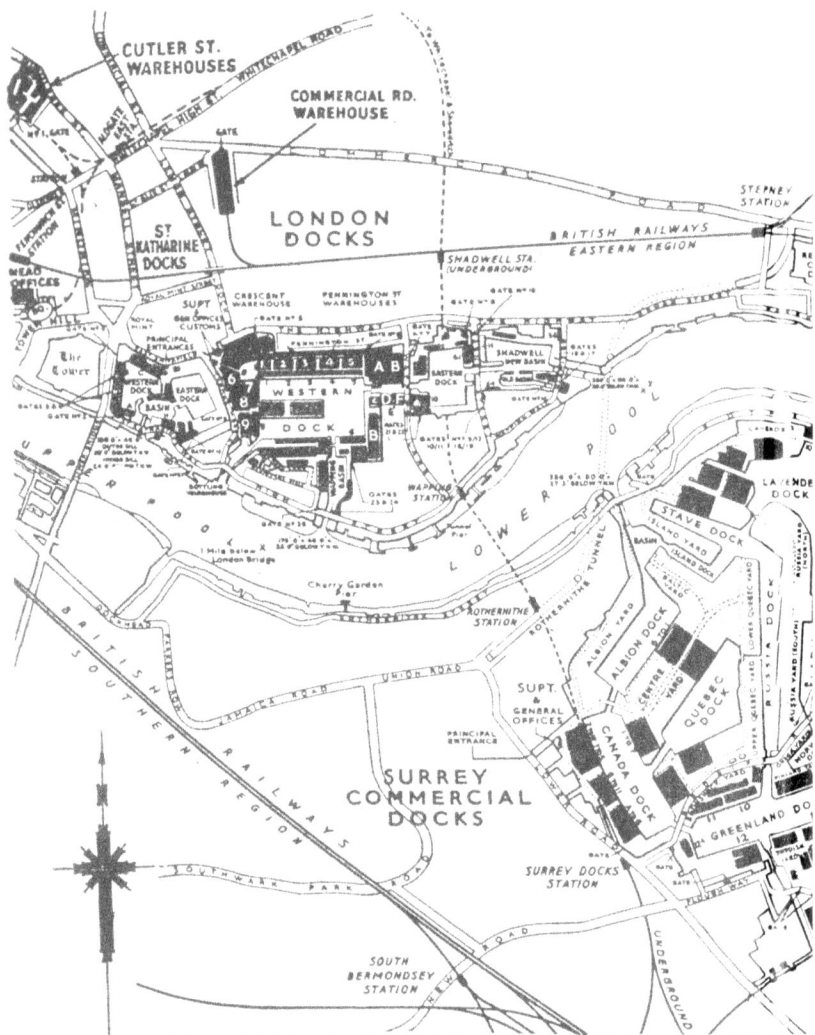

# PORT OF LONDON AUTH

## PLAN OF THE DOCKS

ROAD ACCESS, RAIL CONNECTIONS, SHIPS BERTHS, WAREHOUSES, TRANSIT SH

Scale of Feet

FEET 1000   500   0        1000      2000       3000      4000       5000        6000

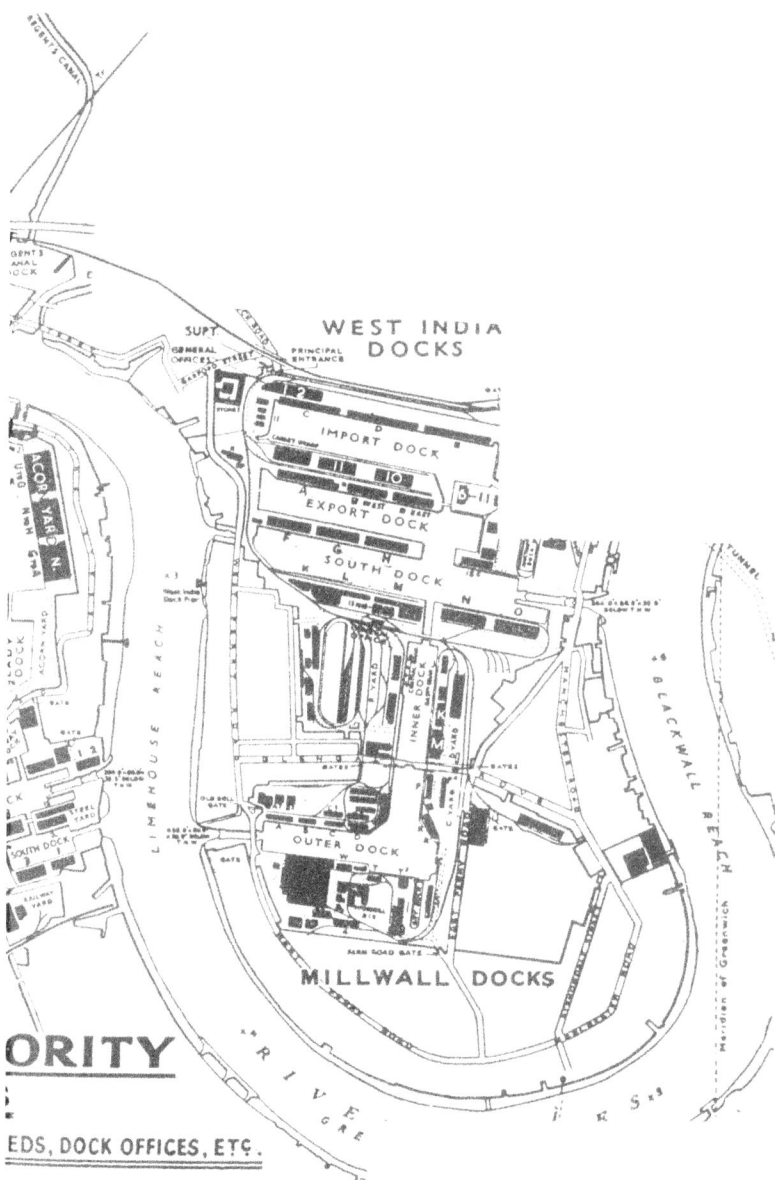

WEST INDIA DOCKS

SUPT

GENERAL OFFICES

PRINCIPAL ENTRANCE

STORES

IMPORT DOCK

EXPORT DOCK

SOUTH DOCK

INNER DOCK

OUTER DOCK

MILLWALL DOCKS

LIMEHOUSE REACH

BLACKWALL REACH

TUNNEL

RIVER

ORITY

EDS, DOCK OFFICES, ETC.

7000    8000 FEET

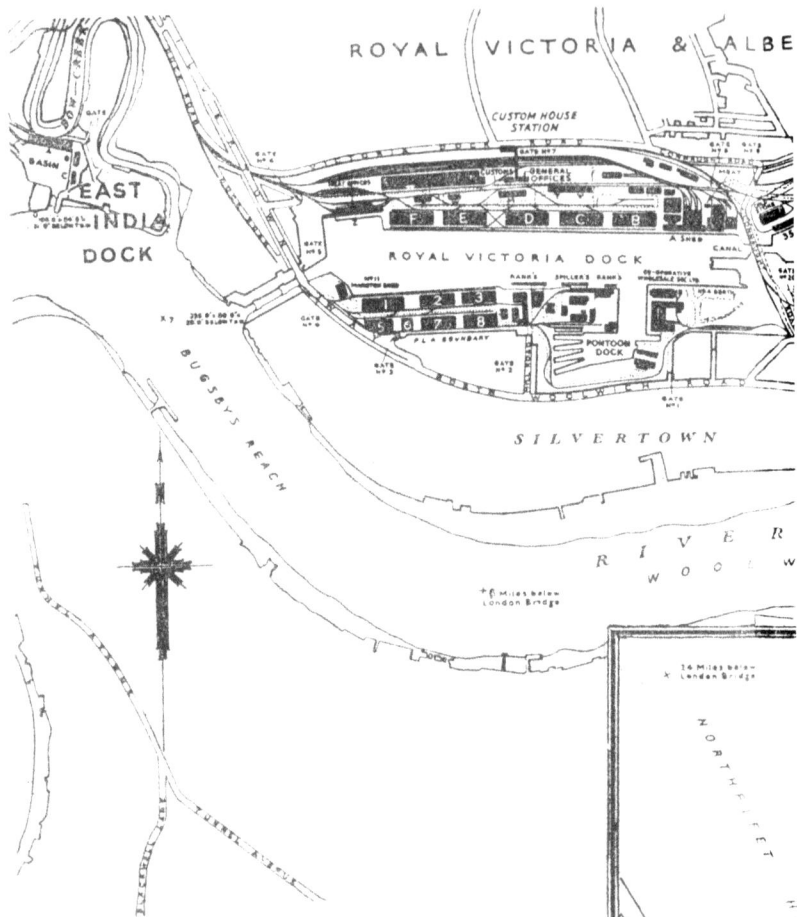

PORT OF LONDON
AUTHORITY
PLAN OF THE DOCKS

ROAD ACCESS, RAIL CONNECTIONS, SHIPS BERTHS,
WAREHOUSES, TRANSIT SHEDS, DOCK OFFICES, ETC.

Scale of feet.

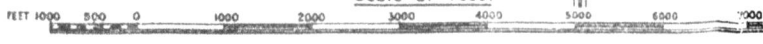

FEET 1000    500    0         1000      2000      3000      4000      5000      6000      7000

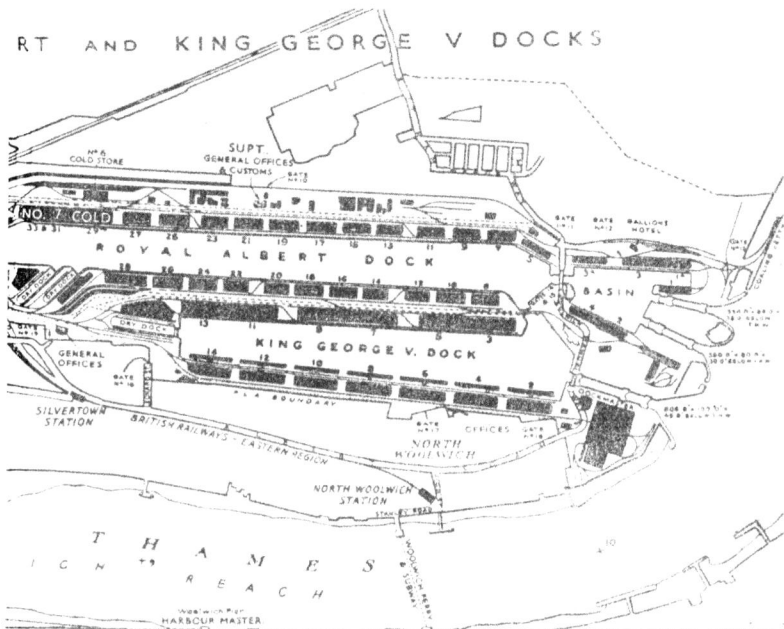

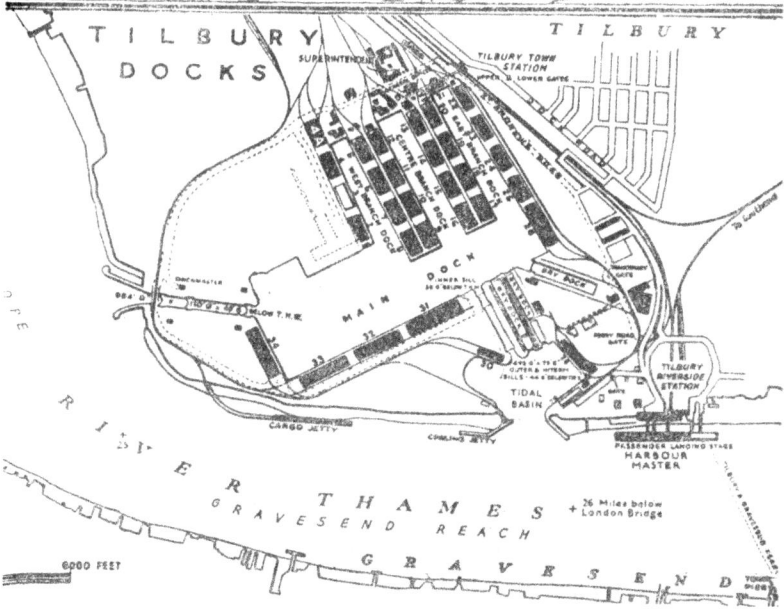

For Product Safety Concerns and Information please contact our EU
representative  GPSR@taylorandfrancis.com
Taylor & Francis Verlag GmbH, Kaufingerstraße 24, 80331 München, Germany

www.ingramcontent.com/pod-product-compliance
Lightning Source LLC
Chambersburg PA
CBHW061215220326
41599CB00025B/4644